TRAVEL THE WORLD ATLAS

WRITTEN BY
Shirley Willis

ILLUSTRATED BY
Nick Hewetson

CREATED AND DESIGNED BY
David Salariya

BOOK HOUSE
a SALARIYA *imprint*

CANADA AND
GREENLAND 10-11

USA: THE WEST AND
MIDWEST 12-13

USA: THE MIDWEST
AND NORTHEAST
14-15

USA: THE SOUTH 16-17

MEXICO, CENTRAL AMERICA AND
THE CARIBBEAN 18-19

SOUTH AMERICA 20-21

Contents

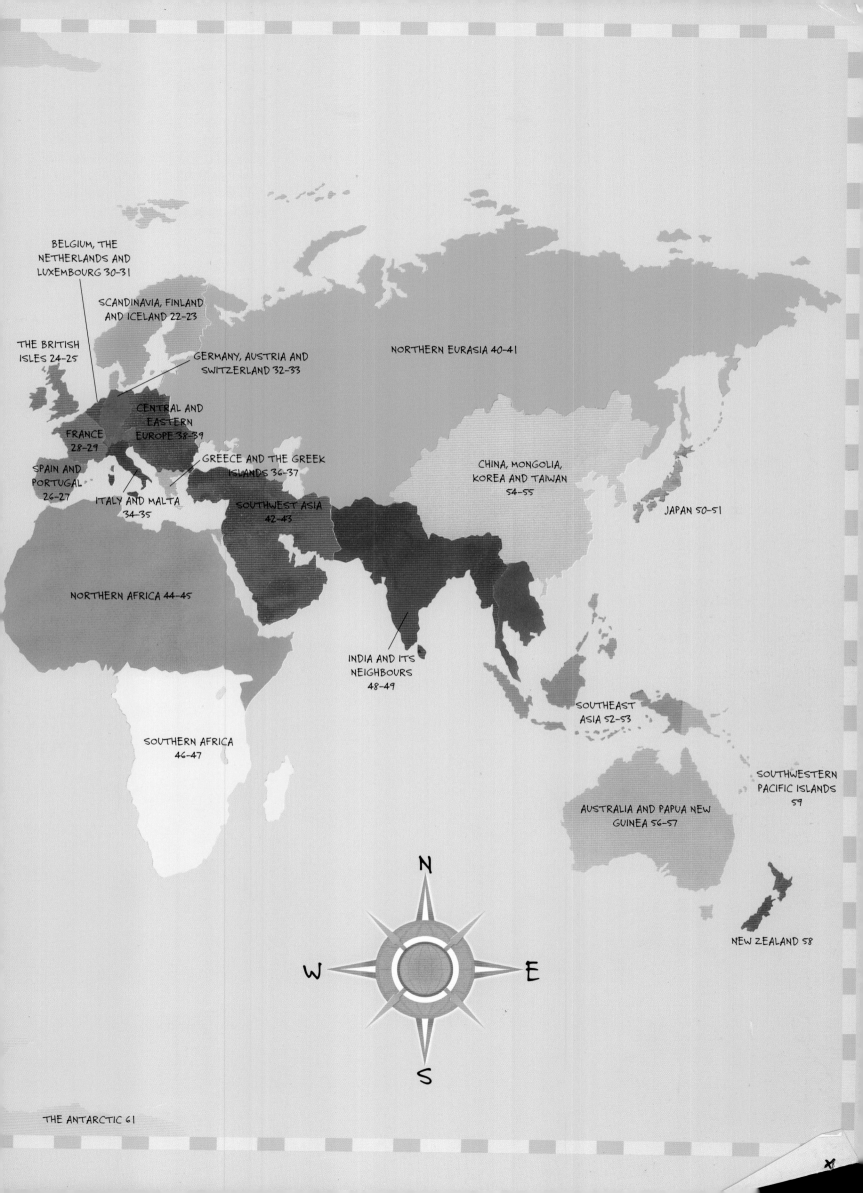

BELGIUM, THE
NETHERLANDS AND
LUXEMBOURG 30-31

SCANDINAVIA, FINLAND
AND ICELAND 22-23

THE BRITISH
ISLES 24-25

GERMANY, AUSTRIA AND
SWITZERLAND 32-33

NORTHERN EURASIA 40-41

CENTRAL AND
EASTERN
EUROPE 38-39

FRANCE
28-29

CHINA, MONGOLIA,
KOREA AND TAIWAN
54-55

SPAIN AND
PORTUGAL
26-27

GREECE AND THE GREEK
ISLANDS 36-37

JAPAN 50-51

ITALY AND MALTA
34-35

SOUTHWEST ASIA
42-43

NORTHERN AFRICA 44-45

INDIA AND ITS
NEIGHBOURS
48-49

SOUTHEAST
ASIA 52-53

SOUTHERN AFRICA
46-47

SOUTHWESTERN
PACIFIC ISLANDS
59

AUSTRALIA AND PAPUA NEW
GUINEA 56-57

N

W   E

NEW ZEALAND 58

S

THE ANTARCTIC 61

The Earth in space

The Earth is a ball of rock that orbits the Sun. It depends on the Sun's energy for warmth and light.

The Earth is one of eight planets that orbit (circle) the Sun. Together they form the Solar System. Each planet orbits the Sun in an elliptical (oval) path. The length of a planet's orbit depends on its distance from the Sun. Mercury is closest and takes 88 days to orbit the Sun, but Neptune takes almost 165 years because it is so far away from the Sun. The Earth's orbit takes about 365 days. Beyond Neptune are 'dwarf' planets such as Pluto.

Neptune

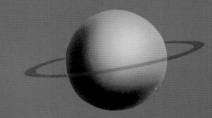

Uranus

Saturn

The Earth is always moving. As it orbits the Sun, the planet spins on its axis, making one complete turn every 24 hours. While one side of its surface is lit by the Sun, the other side is in darkness. This is why we have daytime and night-time.

The Earth's axis is an imaginary line running through its centre.

axis

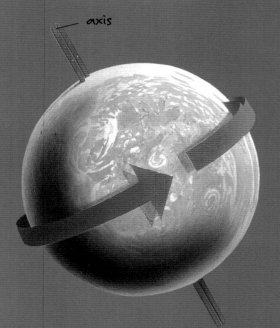

The Earth seen from space

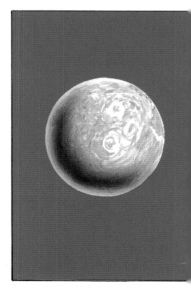

The Earth is 148,800,000 km from the Sun, making it neither too hot nor too cold to live on. It is the only planet in the Solar System where life is known to exist.

Mercury

Venus

Earth

Mars

Sun

Jupiter

From space, the Earth is seen as a huge round ball. The planet looks blue because much of its surface is covered in oceans. Large landmasses, called continents, can also be seen. Closer up, the Earth looks flat. From an aeroplane, the towns, roads, rivers and railway tracks below divide the countryside into a huge patchwork pattern. People are too small to be seen from this distance. If you look down from a skyscraper, people below can be seen but look as small as ants. Cars on the streets look like children's toys.

The Earth seen from an aeroplane

The Earth seen from a tall building

How the world becomes a flat map

A globe is a round map of the world. Map-makers make a flat map of the world for an atlas.

Our planet is made up of four layers (below). We live on the surface of the Earth which is called the crust. Every continent and ocean lies on the Earth's crust. Beneath the crust is a layer of rock called the mantle. Parts of the mantle are hot and molten (liquid) and can break through the crust to form a volcano. The core of the planet has two parts: the outer core is hot, molten metal and the inner core is solid metal.

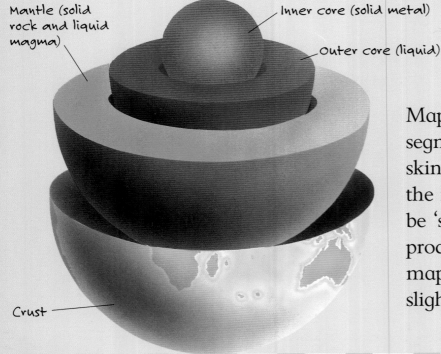

Mantle (solid rock and liquid magma)

Inner core (solid metal)

Outer core (liquid)

Crust

Map-makers divide the world's surface into segments. These are laid side by side like the skin of an orange, but this leaves gaps in the map (above). Parts of the world have to be 'stretched' so that the map joins up. This process is called map projection. On the flat maps in an atlas the countries are shaped slightly differently than they are on a globe.

Map-makers use a grid of imaginary lines across the globe to help plot the exact positions of places. Lines of longitude are drawn from north to south and lines of latitude from east to west.

The equator is an imaginary line dividing the world in half. It is positioned at latitude o (zero degrees). The northern hemisphere is above the equator and the southern hemisphere is below.

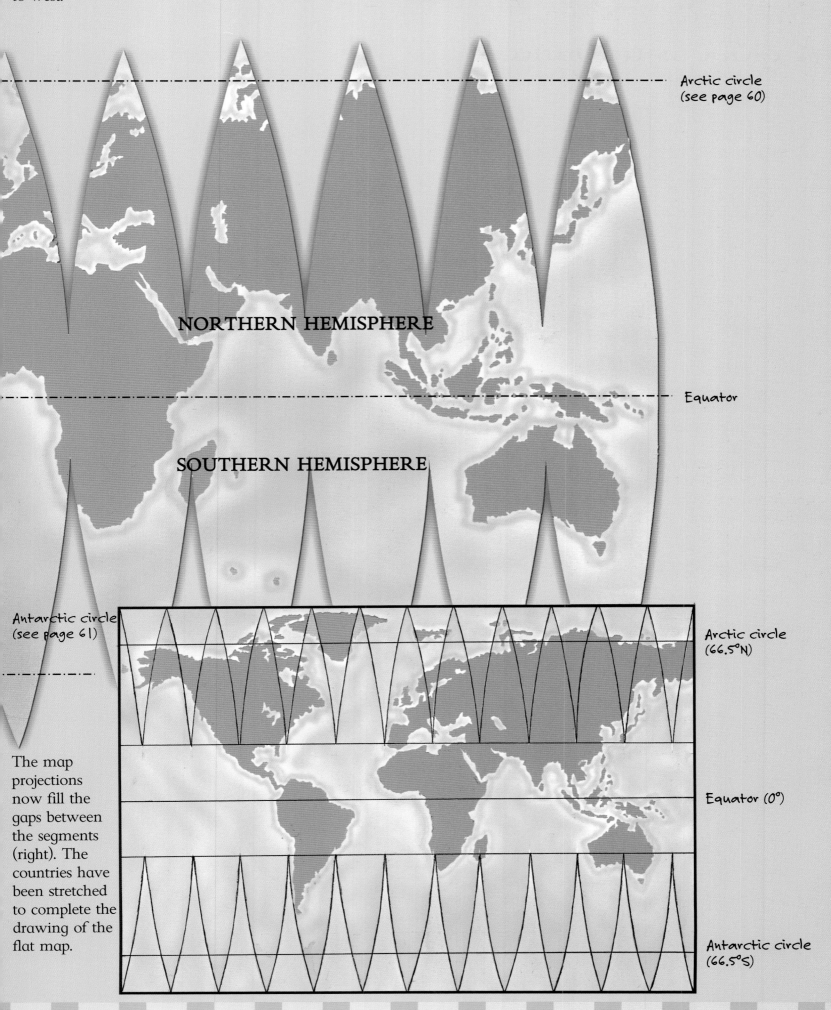

Arctic circle
(see page 60)

NORTHERN HEMISPHERE

Equator

SOUTHERN HEMISPHERE

Antarctic circle
(see page 61)

Arctic circle
(66.5°N)

The map projections now fill the gaps between the segments (right). The countries have been stretched to complete the drawing of the flat map.

Equator (0°)

Antarctic circle
(66.5°S)

How the pages work in this atlas

This is the kind of map you will find in this atlas. Each page shows a map of different countries of the world. The notes on this page explain the type of information given on each map.

'Can you find...' Look at the map to find the buildings or places of interest shown in the box.

A large label in capital letters shows a country's name.

A thick dotted line shows the border between countries. A thin dotted line shows state borders within a country.

The globe shows where each country is in the world.

A small label like this shows the name of a lake or river.

A curved label like this shows the name of a sea or ocean.

Fact boxes give extra information about each country or continent.

Scandinavia, F and Iceland

Norway, Sweden and Denmark are known as Scandinavia. These countries are rich in natural resources: timber, fish, oil and natural gas. They have warm summers but bitterly cold winters.

Can you find...

a stave church?

Legoland?

NORWEG
S

oil rig

stave church

skiing

NORWAY

● BERGEN

fishing boat

ski-jumping

OSLO

Noru
spruc

Drottningholm
Palace

SCANDINAVIA, FINLAND
AND ICELAND

L. Vänern

L. Vättern

● GOTHENBURG

Little
Mermaid

Legoland

DENMARK

Kalmar Castle

NORTH
SEA

COPENHAGEN

GERMANY

Fact:

Hammerfest in Norway is the most northerly town i the world.

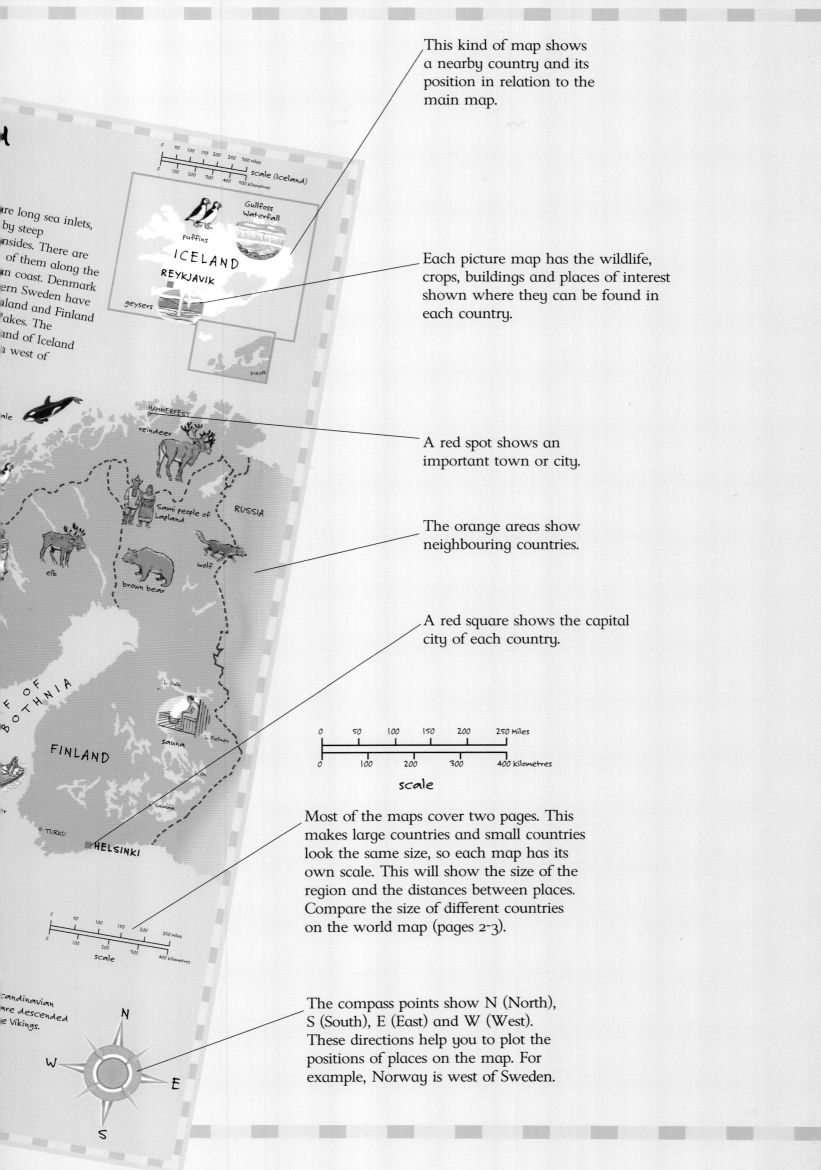

This kind of map shows a nearby country and its position in relation to the main map.

Each picture map has the wildlife, crops, buildings and places of interest shown where they can be found in each country.

A red spot shows an important town or city.

The orange areas show neighbouring countries.

A red square shows the capital city of each country.

Most of the maps cover two pages. This makes large countries and small countries look the same size, so each map has its own scale. This will show the size of the region and the distances between places. Compare the size of different countries on the world map (pages 2-3).

The compass points show N (North), S (South), E (East) and W (West). These directions help you to plot the positions of places on the map. For example, Norway is west of Sweden.

re long sea inlets, by steep nsides. There are of them along the n coast. Denmark ern Sweden have land and Finland akes. The nd of Iceland n west of

candinavian ve descended e Vikings.

ICELAND
REYKJAVIK
puffins
Gullfoss Waterfall
geysers

scale (Iceland)

EUROPE

HAMMERFEST
reindeer
Sami people of Lapland
RUSSIA
elk
brown bear
wolf

F OF BOTHNIA
FINLAND
L. Oulu
sauna
L. Pielinen
L. Ori
L. Saimaa
TURKU
HELSINKI

scale

scale

Canada and Greenland

Canada is the second biggest country in the world but it does not have a large population. Few people live in northern Canada as the climate there is too cold.

Canada has two official languages: English and French. Montreal (above) in Quebec is the largest French-speaking city in the world after Paris.

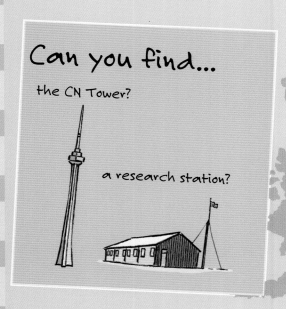

Can you find...

the CN Tower?

a research station?

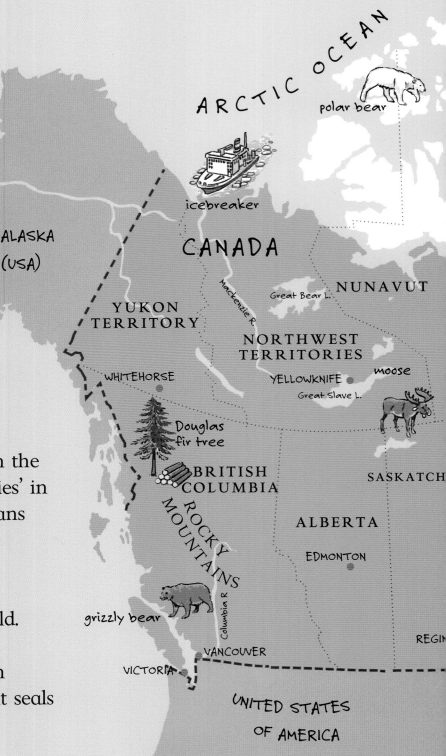

ARCTIC OCEAN

polar bear

icebreaker

ALASKA (USA)

CANADA

Mackenzie R.

Great Bear L.

NUNAVUT

YUKON TERRITORY

NORTHWEST TERRITORIES

WHITEHORSE

YELLOWKNIFE

Great Slave L.

moose

PACIFIC OCEAN

Douglas fir tree

BRITISH COLUMBIA

SASKATCH

ROCKY MOUNTAINS

ALBERTA

EDMONTON

grizzly bear

Columbia R

REGIN

VANCOUVER

VICTORIA

UNITED STATES OF AMERICA

There are high, rocky mountain ranges in the west and rich, flat farmlands called 'prairies' in the central area of Canada. Most Canadians live in the big cities in the east where the climate is less cold.

Greenland is the largest island in the world. It belongs to Denmark but has its own government. The Inuit people who live in northern Canada and Greenland still hunt seals and polar bears.

scale

0 100 200 300 400 500 600 Miles

0 200 400 600 800 1000 Kilometres

Toronto's CN Tower is one of the tallest buildings in the world — it is 553 m tall.

N

W E

S

research station

snowmobile

polar bear

GREENLAND

(KALAALLIT NUNAAT) (DENMARK)

BAFFIN BAY

igloo

research station

fishing boat

BAFFIN ISLAND

iceberg

NUUK

LABRADOR SEA

CANADA AND GREENLAND

elephant seal

Inuit people

killer whale

wolves

NEWFOUNDLAND AND LABRADOR

HUDSON BAY

QUEBEC

ST JOHN'S

beaver

Nelson R.

Château Frontenac

PRINCE EDWARD ISLAND

CHARLOTTETOWN

ATLANTIC OCEAN

MANITOBA

ONTARIO

Parliament Buildings

QUEBEC CITY

NOVA SCOTIA

HALIFAX

Mountie

WINNIPEG

L. Superior

CN Tower

MONTREAL

OTTAWA

FREDERICTON

NEW BRUNSWICK

Fact:

Hudson Bay is frozen over for six months every year.

L. Huron

L. Ontario

TORONTO

Niagara Falls

L. Michigan

L. Erie

USA: The West and Midwest

The United States of America (USA) is one of the wealthiest countries in the world. It is made up of fifty states. The western states include Alaska in the far north and Hawaii, 4,000 km out in the Pacific Ocean.

The rugged landscape of the western states is dominated by the Rocky Mountains. California is the largest state in the region. More people live there than in any other American state.

PACIFIC OCEAN

SEATTLE
OLYMPIA
WASHINGTON

Columbia R.

PORTLAND
SALEM

OREGON

redwood tree

BOISE

Golden Gate Bridge

NEVADA

RENO
CARSON CITY

SACRAMENTO

SAN FRANCISCO

wild horses

CALIFORNIA

grey whale

LAS VEGAS
L. Mead

HOLLYWOOD

LOS ANGELES

SAN DIEGO

Colorado R.

0	100	200	300 Miles	
scale
0	100	200	300	400	500 Kilometres

PACIFIC OCEAN

caribou

walrus

ALASKA

ANCHORAGE

whale

JUNEAU

0	200	400	600 Miles
0	200	400	600	800	1000 Kilometres

scale (Alaska)

NORTH AMERICA

N
W   E
S

Hamburgers were invented in the USA and are now eaten all over the world.

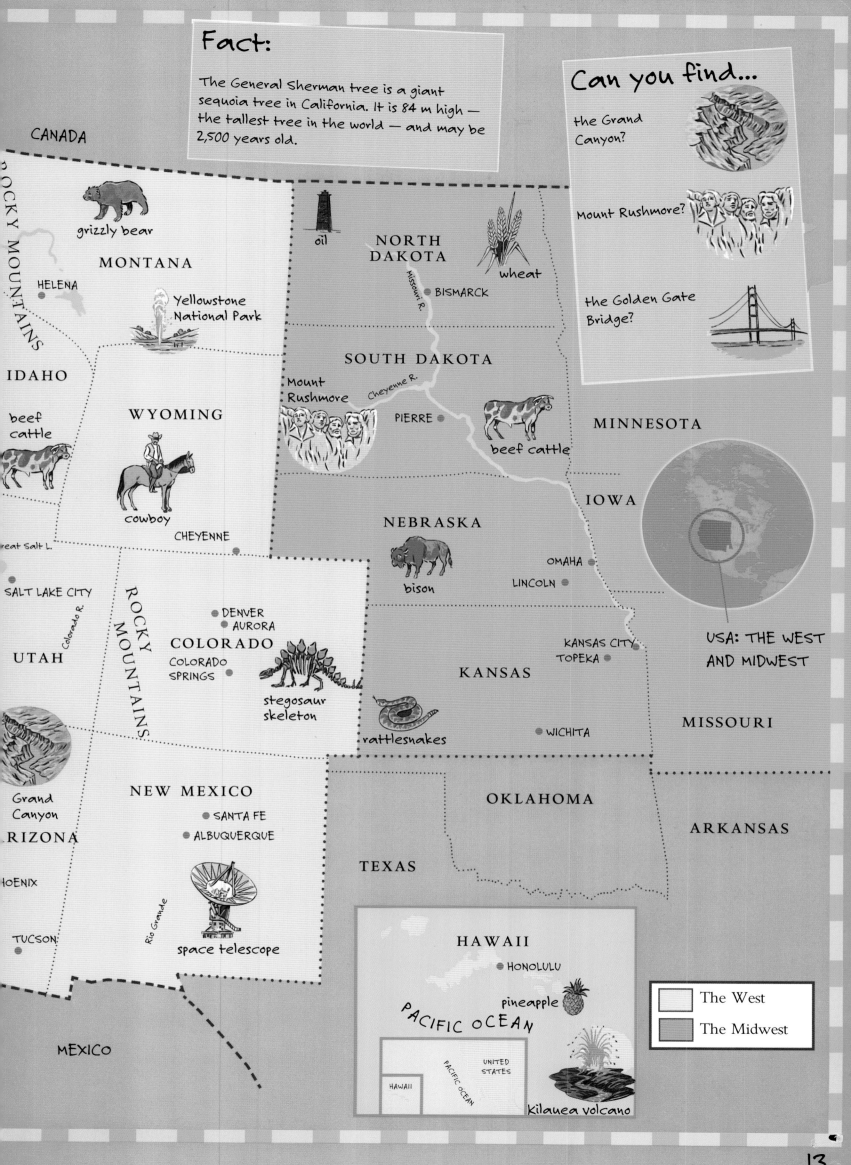

Fact:

The General Sherman tree is a giant sequoia tree in California. It is 84 m high — the tallest tree in the world — and may be 2,500 years old.

CANADA

grizzly bear

MONTANA

HELENA

Yellowstone National Park

oil

NORTH DAKOTA

Missouri R.

BISMARCK

wheat

Can you find...

the Grand Canyon?

Mount Rushmore?

the Golden Gate Bridge?

ROCKY MOUNTAINS

IDAHO

beef cattle

WYOMING

cowboy

CHEYENNE

SOUTH DAKOTA

Mount Rushmore

Cheyenne R.

PIERRE

beef cattle

MINNESOTA

IOWA

Great Salt L.

SALT LAKE CITY

UTAH

Colorado R.

ROCKY MOUNTAINS

DENVER
AURORA

COLORADO

COLORADO SPRINGS

stegosaur skeleton

NEBRASKA

bison

OMAHA

LINCOLN

KANSAS CITY
TOPEKA

KANSAS

rattlesnakes

WICHITA

USA: THE WEST AND MIDWEST

MISSOURI

Grand Canyon

ARIZONA

PHOENIX

NEW MEXICO

SANTA FE

ALBUQUERQUE

Rio Grande

space telescope

TUCSON

OKLAHOMA

TEXAS

ARKANSAS

HAWAII

HONOLULU

pineapple

PACIFIC OCEAN

MEXICO

UNITED STATES

HAWAII

PACIFIC OCEAN

Kilauea volcano

The West

The Midwest

13

USA: The Midwest and Northeast

The United States is the world's most industrialised country. The area around the Great Lakes supplies most of the USA's iron and steel. Detroit was famous as the centre of the American car industry.

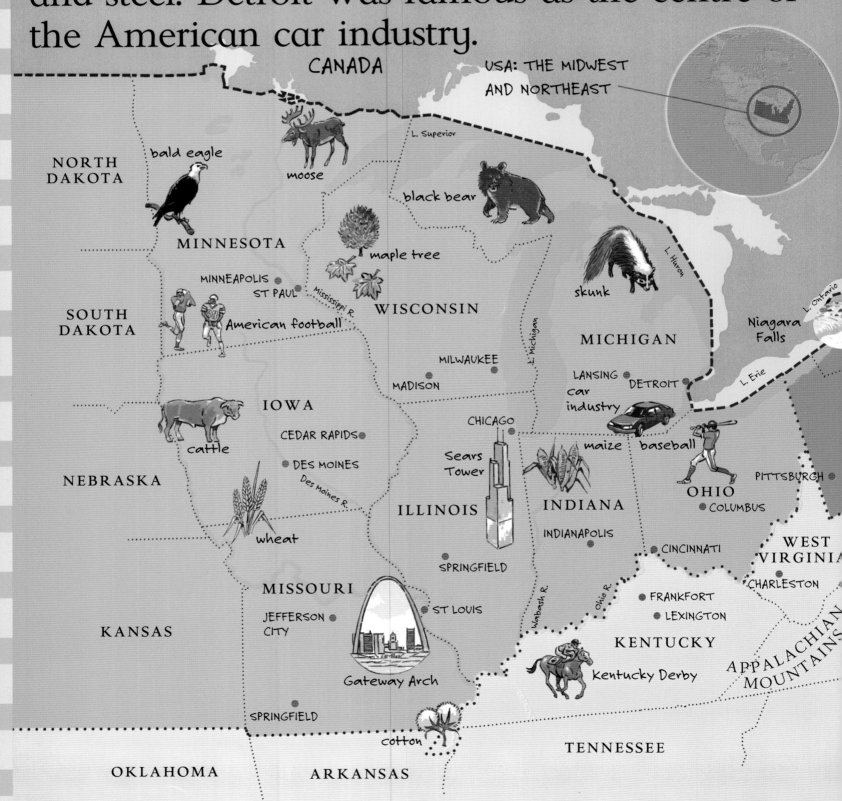

CANADA

USA: THE MIDWEST AND NORTHEAST

L. Superior

NORTH DAKOTA

bald eagle

moose

black bear

MINNESOTA

maple tree

L. Huron

skunk

L. Ontario

MINNEAPOLIS
ST PAUL

Mississippi R.

WISCONSIN

SOUTH DAKOTA

American football

MICHIGAN

L. Michigan

Niagara Falls

MILWAUKEE

LANSING

DETROIT

L. Erie

MADISON

car industry

IOWA

CEDAR RAPIDS

cattle

CHICAGO

maize

baseball

DES MOINES

Sears Tower

NEBRASKA

Des Moines R.

PITTSBURGH

ILLINOIS

INDIANA

OHIO

COLUMBUS

wheat

INDIANAPOLIS

SPRINGFIELD

CINCINNATI

WEST VIRGINIA

MISSOURI

St LOUIS

Wabash R.

Ohio R.

FRANKFORT

CHARLESTON

JEFFERSON CITY

LEXINGTON

KANSAS

KENTUCKY

APPALACHIAN MOUNTAINS

Gateway Arch

Kentucky Derby

SPRINGFIELD

cotton

TENNESSEE

OKLAHOMA

ARKANSAS

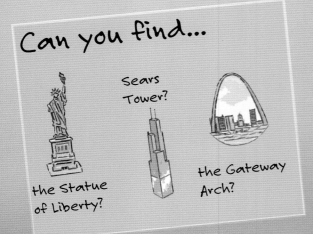

Can you find...

Sears Tower?

the Statue of Liberty?

the Gateway Arch?

The flat, fertile plains south of the Great Lakes produce so much wheat and maize that the area is known as the 'breadbasket of the world'. Over the Appalachian Mountains lie the great cities of the Atlantic coast. New York City is the largest city in the USA, with a population of 8.5 million.

Fact:

The White House in Washington, D.C. (District of Columbia) has been the home of United States presidents for nearly 200 years.

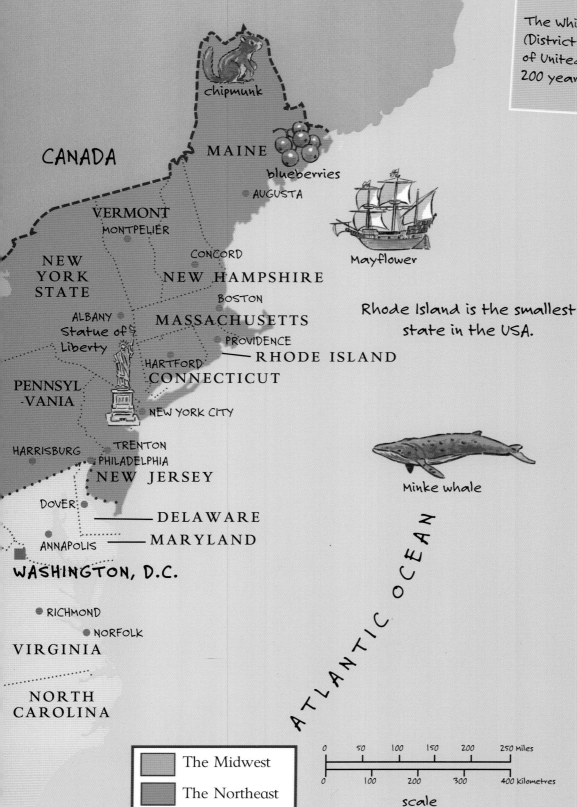

chipmunk

CANADA

MAINE

blueberries

AUGUSTA

VERMONT

MONTPELIER

CONCORD

NEW YORK STATE

NEW HAMPSHIRE

BOSTON

ALBANY

MASSACHUSETTS

Statue of Liberty

PROVIDENCE

RHODE ISLAND

HARTFORD

CONNECTICUT

PENNSYL -VANIA

NEW YORK CITY

HARRISBURG

TRENTON

PHILADELPHIA

NEW JERSEY

DOVER

DELAWARE

ANNAPOLIS

MARYLAND

WASHINGTON, D.C.

RICHMOND

NORFOLK

VIRGINIA

NORTH CAROLINA

Mayflower

Rhode Island is the smallest state in the USA.

Minke whale

ATLANTIC OCEAN

The Statue of Liberty was built by Gustave Eiffel in Paris, France. It was shipped to America in pieces and put together there. A staircase inside its hollow structure allows visitors to climb up to Liberty's crown.

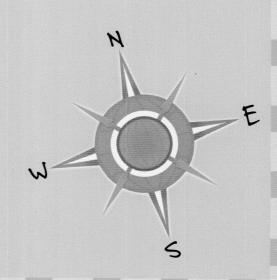

N

E

W

S

| | The Midwest |
| | The Northeast |

0   50   100   150   200   250 Miles

0   100   200   300   400 Kilometres

scale

15

USA: The South

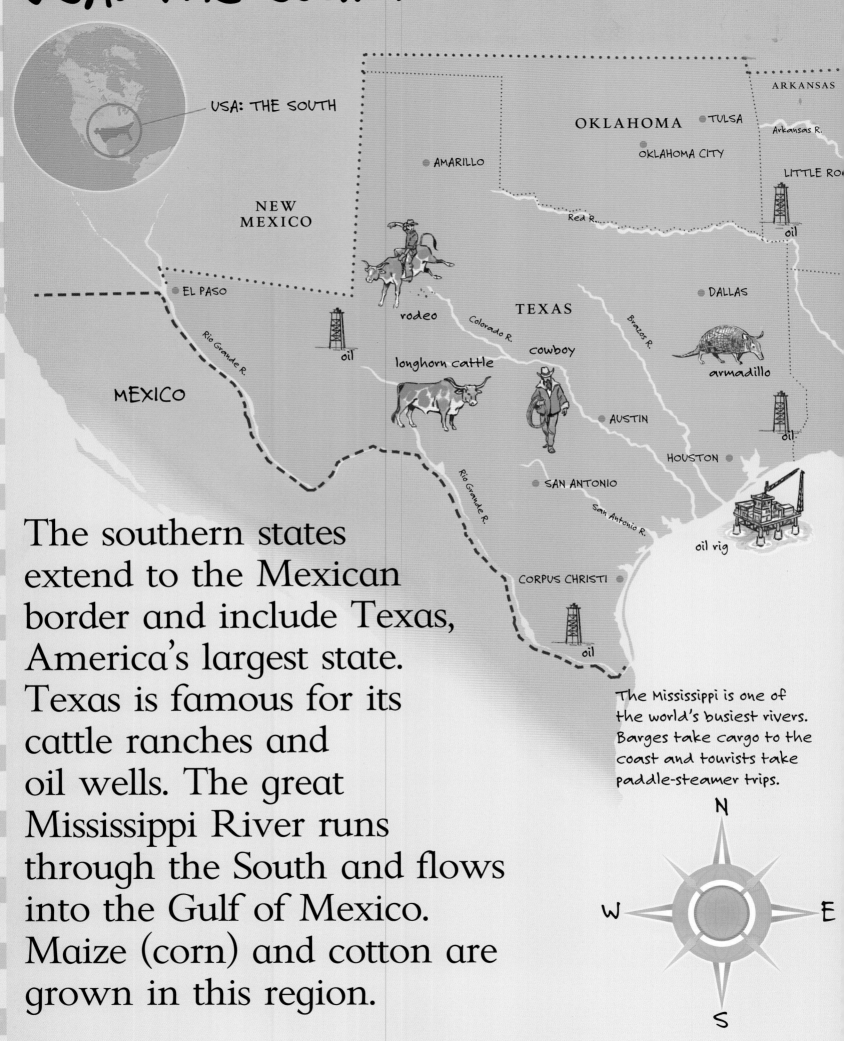

USA: THE SOUTH

ARKANSAS

OKLAHOMA
TULSA
Arkansas R.
OKLAHOMA CITY
AMARILLO
LITTLE RO[C]
oil

NEW MEXICO

Red R.

rodeo

EL PASO

Colorado R.
TEXAS
Brazos R.
DALLAS

Rio Grande R.

oil

longhorn cattle

cowboy

armadillo

MEXICO

AUSTIN

oil

HOUSTON

Rio Grande R.

SAN ANTONIO

San Antonio R.

oil rig

CORPUS CHRISTI

oil

The southern states extend to the Mexican border and include Texas, America's largest state. Texas is famous for its cattle ranches and oil wells. The great Mississippi River runs through the South and flows into the Gulf of Mexico. Maize (corn) and cotton are grown in this region.

The Mississippi is one of the world's busiest rivers. Barges take cargo to the coast and tourists take paddle-steamer trips.

N
W   E
S

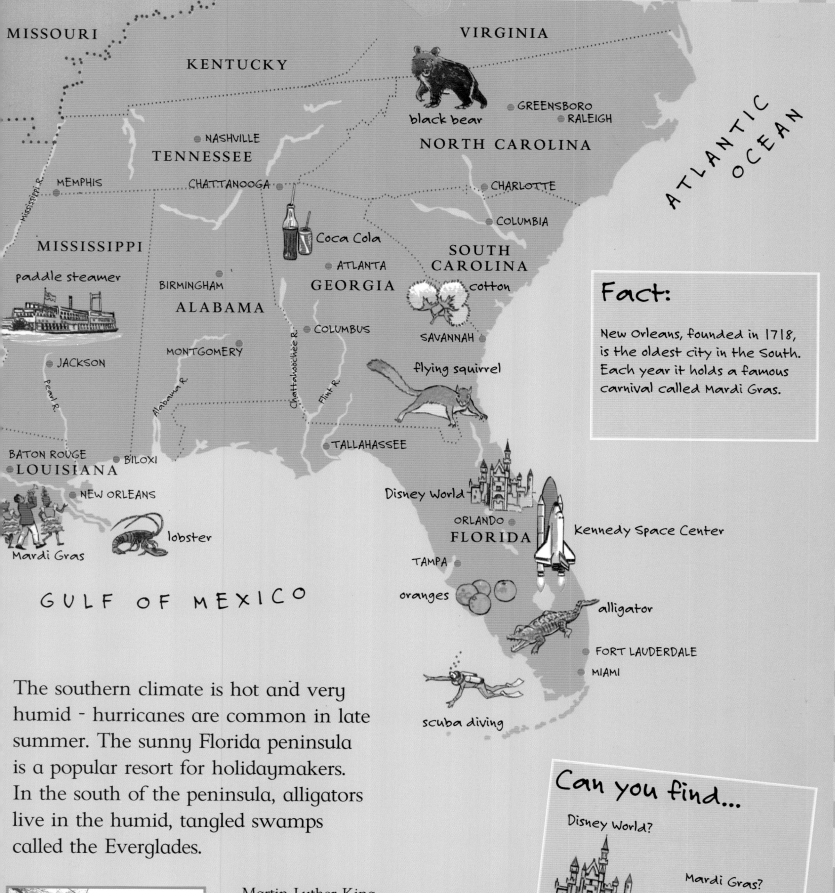

MISSOURI

VIRGINIA

KENTUCKY

black bear

GREENSBORO
RALEIGH

NASHVILLE

NORTH CAROLINA

TENNESSEE

MEMPHIS

CHATTANOOGA

CHARLOTTE

COLUMBIA

Coca Cola

MISSISSIPPI

SOUTH
CAROLINA

paddle steamer

BIRMINGHAM

ATLANTA
GEORGIA

cotton

ALABAMA

COLUMBUS

SAVANNAH

JACKSON

MONTGOMERY

flying squirrel

ATLANTIC OCEAN

TALLAHASSEE

BATON ROUGE
LOUISIANA

BILOXI

Disney World

NEW ORLEANS

lobster

ORLANDO
FLORIDA

Kennedy Space Center

Mardi Gras

TAMPA

GULF OF MEXICO

oranges

alligator

FORT LAUDERDALE

MIAMI

scuba diving

Fact:

New Orleans, founded in 1718, is the oldest city in the South. Each year it holds a famous carnival called Mardi Gras.

The southern climate is hot and very humid - hurricanes are common in late summer. The sunny Florida peninsula is a popular resort for holidaymakers. In the south of the peninsula, alligators live in the humid, tangled swamps called the Everglades.

Martin Luther King, an American civil rights leader, was born in this house in Atlanta, Georgia.

Can you find...

Disney World?

Mardi Gras?

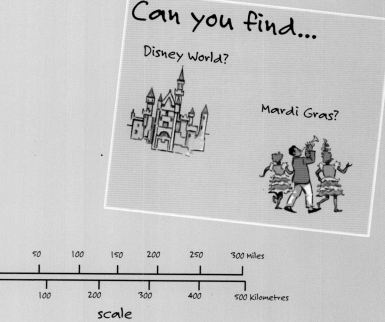

| 0 | 50 | 100 | 150 | 200 | 250 | 300 Miles |

| 0 | 100 | 200 | 300 | 400 | 500 Kilometres |

scale

Mexico, Central America and the Caribbean

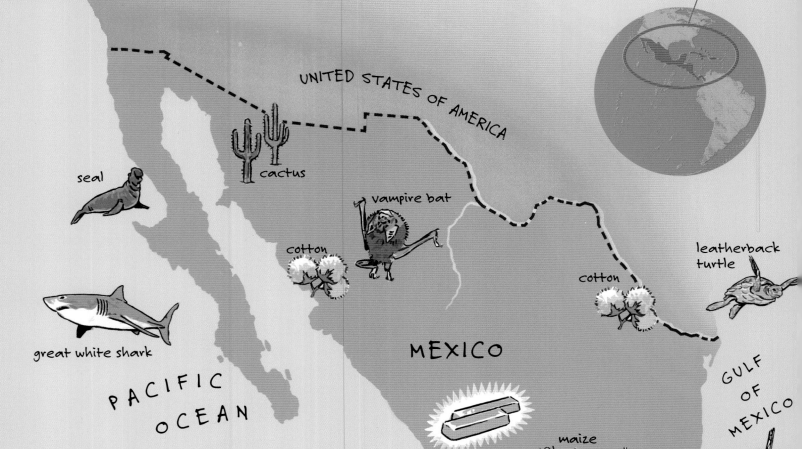

MEXICO, CENTRAL AMERICA AND THE CARIBBEAN

UNITED STATES OF AMERICA

seal

cactus

vampire bat

cotton

cotton

leatherback turtle

great white shark

PACIFIC OCEAN

MEXICO

GULF OF MEXICO

gold

maize

oil rig

National Cathedral

MEXICO CITY

Olmec stone heads

dolphin

ACAPULCO

Mexico and Central America link the continents of North and South America. The land is mountainous and much of it is covered by tropical rainforests. The Panama Canal, in the south of the region, provides a link for ships between the Atlantic and Pacific Oceans.

Can you find...

Chichén Itzá?

the Olmec stone heads?

the National Cathedral?

Mexico is this region's largest country. It is rich in silver and oil. Bananas and coffee grow in Central America and the Caribbean. The warm seas and climate of the Caribbean's volcanic islands attract many tourists. This region is a hurricane zone. Fierce tropical storms around the Gulf of Mexico create enormous waves that can cause a lot of damage.

Fact:

Mexico City is slowly sinking each year because it is built on the bed of an ancient lake.

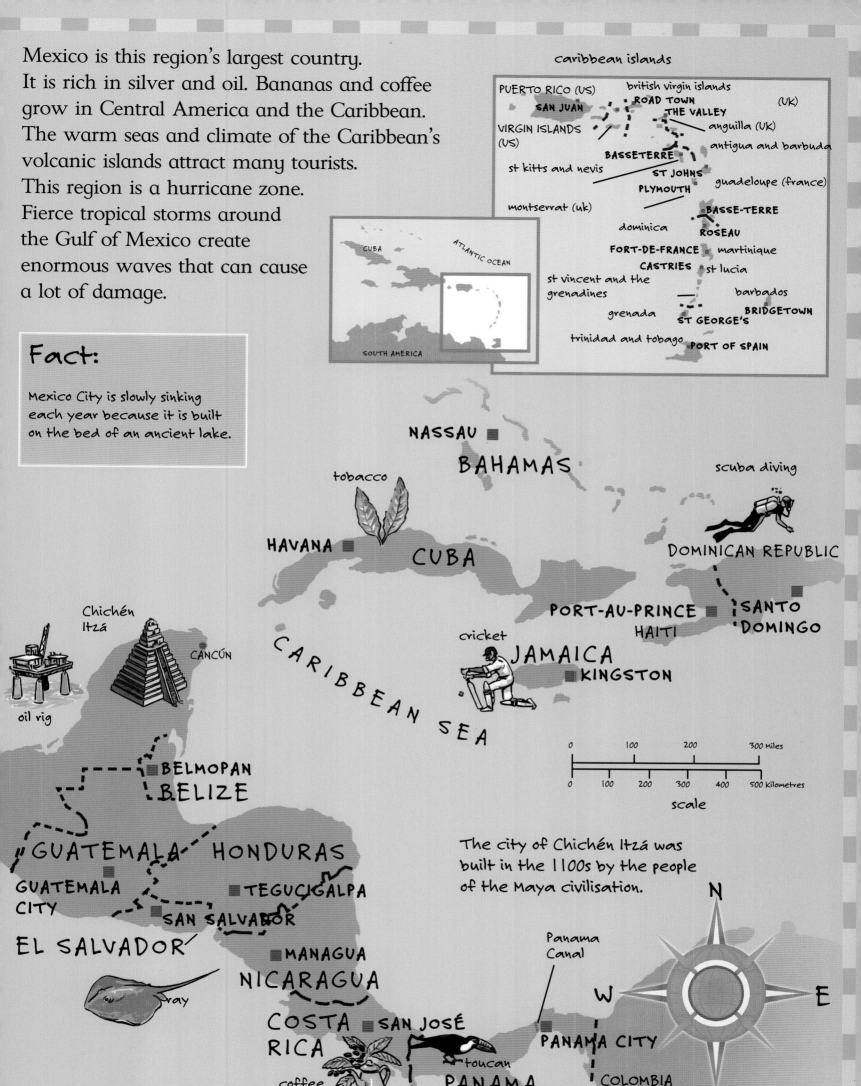

caribbean islands

PUERTO RICO (US)
SAN JUAN
VIRGIN ISLANDS (US)
british virgin islands
ROAD TOWN
THE VALLEY (UK)
anguilla (UK)
antigua and barbuda
BASSETERRE
st kitts and nevis
ST JOHNS
PLYMOUTH
guadeloupe (france)
montserrat (uk)
BASSE-TERRE
dominica
ROSEAU
FORT-DE-FRANCE martinique
CASTRIES st lucia
st vincent and the grenadines
barbados
grenada
ST GEORGE'S
BRIDGETOWN
trinidad and tobago
PORT OF SPAIN

CUBA
ATLANTIC OCEAN
SOUTH AMERICA

NASSAU
BAHAMAS
tobacco
scuba diving
HAVANA
CUBA
DOMINICAN REPUBLIC
PORT-AU-PRINCE
HAITI
SANTO DOMINGO
cricket
JAMAICA
KINGSTON

CARIBBEAN SEA

Chichén Itzá
CANCÚN
oil rig

BELMOPAN
BELIZE

GUATEMALA HONDURAS
GUATEMALA CITY
TEGUCIGALPA
SAN SALVADOR
EL SALVADOR
ray
MANAGUA
NICARAGUA
COSTA RICA
SAN JOSÉ
toucan
coffee
PANAMA
Panama Canal
PANAMA CITY
COLOMBIA

0 100 200 300 Miles
0 100 200 300 400 500 Kilometres
scale

The city of Chichén Itzá was built in the 1100s by the people of the Maya civilisation.

N
W E
S

South America

Machu Picchu was a holy city, built by the Inca civilisation in the 15th century. The ancient mountain-top settlement in the Peruvian Andes was rediscovered in 1911.

SOUTH AMERICA

Tomatoes were first discovered growing in South America.

N
E
W
S

scale

| | | | | | | | | | | |
| 0 | 100 | 200 | 300 | 400 | 500 | 600 miles |

| 0 | 200 | 400 | 600 | 800 | 1000 kilometres |

30 miles

0   25   50 kilometres

0

scale (Galápagos Islands)

ATLANTIC OCEAN

green turtle

CARACAS

VENEZUELA

Angel Falls

GUYANA

GEORGETOWN

PARAMARIBO

SURINAME

CAYENNE

FRENCH GUIANA (FRANCE)

Ariane rocket launch site

PANAMA

COLOMBIA

BOGOTÁ

coffee

QUITO

EQUADOR

jaguar

tarantula

Machu Picchu

PERU

piranha

anaconda

Xingu R.

Tapajós R.

Amazon R.

Ucayali R.

rainforest

BRAZIL

NATAL

GALÁPAGOS ISLANDS (ECUADOR)

SOUTH AMERICA

giant tortoise

marine iguana

20

BRASÍLIA

Brasília Cathedral

Sugarloaf Mountain

RIO DE JANEIRO

Statue of Christ

ATLANTIC OCEAN

diamond

PARAGUAY
ASUNCIÓN

URUGUAY
MONTEVIDEO

LA PAZ
BOLIVIA
SUCRE

Andean condor

llama

ANDES

BUENOS AIRES
ARGENTINA

SANTIAGO

volcano

cattle

CHILE

oil

sheep

oil

FALKLAND ISLANDS (UK)
STANLEY

The Andes mountains run the length of the huge continent of South America. In the north, the Amazon River runs through vast tropical rainforests full of wildlife. In the south, millions of cattle and sheep are reared on fertile grasslands called Pampas.

South America is rich in oil, silver, copper, coal and iron ore. The continent's largest country, Brazil, is also the richest and most industrialised and is the world's leading coffee producer. Spanish is spoken throughout South America except in Brazil, where the language is Portuguese.

Fact:

Angel Falls in Venezuela is the highest waterfall in the world at over 800 m.

Can you find...

Angel Falls?

the Statue of Christ?

Machu Picchu?

Scandinavia, Finland and Iceland

Norway, Sweden and Denmark are known as Scandinavia. These countries are rich in natural resources: timber, fish, oil and natural gas. They have warm summers but bitterly cold winters.

Fjords are long sea inlets, banked by steep mountainsides. There are hundreds of them along the Norwegian coast. Denmark and southern Sweden have fertile farmland and Finland has many lakes. The volcanic island of Iceland lies 1,000 km west of Norway.

scale (Iceland)

0 50 100 150 200 250 300 miles

0 100 200 300 400 500 kilometres

Gulfoss Waterfall

puffins

ICELAND

REYKJAVIK

geysers

EUROPE

RUSSIA

wolf

Sami people of Lapland

brown bear

reindeer

HAMMERFEST

elk

killer whale

puffins

ice hockey

NORWEGIAN SEA

Can you find...

Legoland?

a stave church?

SCANDINAVIA, FINLAND AND ICELAND

FINLAND

L. Oulu
L. Pielinen
L. Ovi
L. Saimaa

sauna

HELSINKI

TURKU

ice-breaker

SWEDEN

GULF OF BOTHNIA

L. Stor

Norwegian spruce

Drottningholm Palace

UPPSALA

STOCKHOLM

skiing

ski-jumping

NORWAY

OSLO

stave church

BERGEN

oil rig

fishing boat

L. Vänern

L. Vättern

GOTHENBURG

Kalmar Castle

BALTIC SEA

Little Mermaid

Legoland

COPENHAGEN

DENMARK

GERMANY

NORTH SEA

scale

0   50   100   150   200   250 miles

0   100   200   300   400 kilometres

N
W   E
S

The Scandinavian people are descended from the Vikings.

Fact:

Hammerfest in Norway is the most northerly town in the world.

23

The British Isles

The United Kingdom (UK) and Ireland are known as the British Isles. Much of the land is farmed, but there are many large cities. London, the biggest city and the capital of the UK, is a major financial and cultural centre.
The Channel Tunnel links the UK with mainland Europe.

Fact:

The Forth Bridge, Scotland, was the first major bridge in the world to be built of steel.

THE BRITISH ISLES

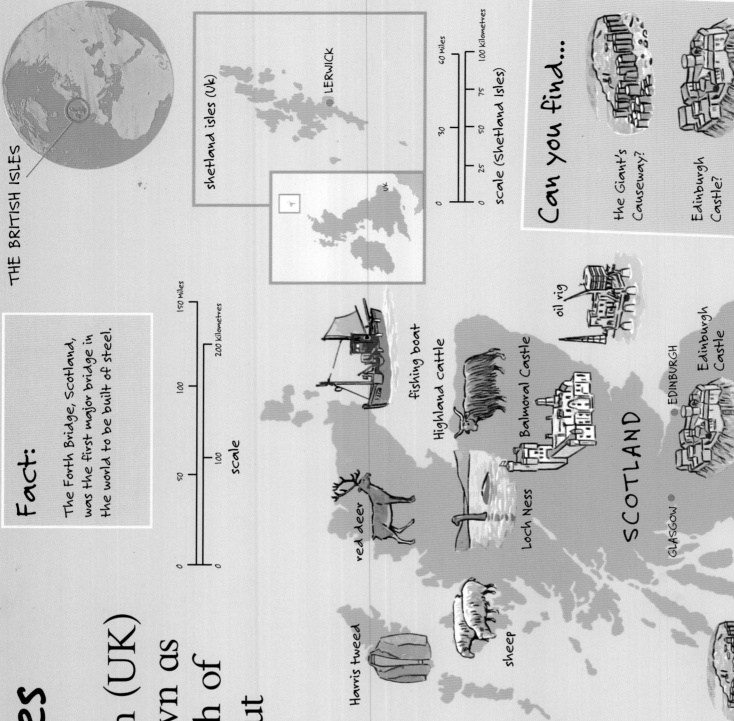

scale

0   50   100   150 miles
0   100   200 kilometres

Shetland isles (Vk)

LERWICK

scale (Shetland Isles)

0   25   50   75   100 kilometres
0   30   60 miles

UK

Can you find...

the Giant's Causeway?

Edinburgh Castle?

oil rig

fishing boat

Highland cattle

Balmoral Castle

red deer

Loch Ness

SCOTLAND

GLASGOW

EDINBURGH

Edinburgh Castle

Hadrian's Wall

Harris tweed

sheep

Giant's Causeway

NORTHERN IRELAND

ATLANTIC OCEAN

NORTH SEA

UNITED KINGDOM

YORK

Castle Howard

MANCHESTER

LIVERPOOL

Trent R.

ENGLAND

WALES

Shakespeare's birthplace

STRATFORD-UPON-AVON

Severn R.

CARDIFF

Stonehenge

Tower of London

Thames R.

LONDON

Big Ben

Brighton Pavilion

BRIGHTON

DOVER

Channel Tunnel

Brighton

cross-Channel ferry

PLYMOUTH

ENGLISH CHANNEL

IRISH SEA

DUBLIN

REPUBLIC OF IRELAND

Shannon R.

horses

lobster

lobster

CORK

crystal

England, Scotland, Wales and Northern Ireland form the United Kingdom. England is the most densely populated of these countries.

Southern Ireland is not part of the UK. It is called the Republic of Ireland. Most of its industries are based around Dublin and Cork.

The Channel Tunnel links Folkestone in England with Calais in France and is nearly 50 km long.

channel islands

guernsey (UK)

ST PETER PORT

ENGLISH CHANNEL

Jersey (UK)

ST HELIER

scale (Channel Islands)

0   15   30 miles

0   10   20   30   40   50 kilometres

UK

ENGLISH CHANNEL

N

W   E

S

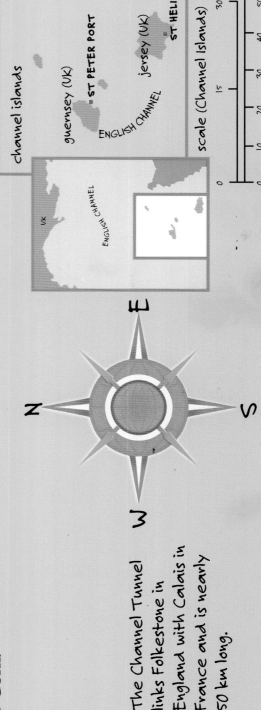

The Tower of London is world-famous. The British crown jewels used at coronations and other state occasions are kept there.

25

Spain and Portugal

Madrid is the highest capital city in Europe at 640 m above sea level.

ATLANTIC OCEAN

Spain and Portugal form the Iberian Peninsula. They are separated from the rest of Europe by the Pyrenees mountains. Most of the peninsula is dry grassland with olive groves. This region is dry and hot in summer.

maize

brown bear

port

OPORTO

PORTUGAL

House of Shells

Tagus R.

LISBON

olives

oranges

cork trees

lynx

SEVILLE

sherry

Rock of Gibraltar

GIBRALTAR (UK)

MOROCCO

Antoní Gaudi began work on Barcelona's famous church, the Sagrada Familia, in 1883. The building work still continues today because the church has not yet been completed.

0	25	50	75	100	125 Miles
0	50		100	150	200 kilometres

scale

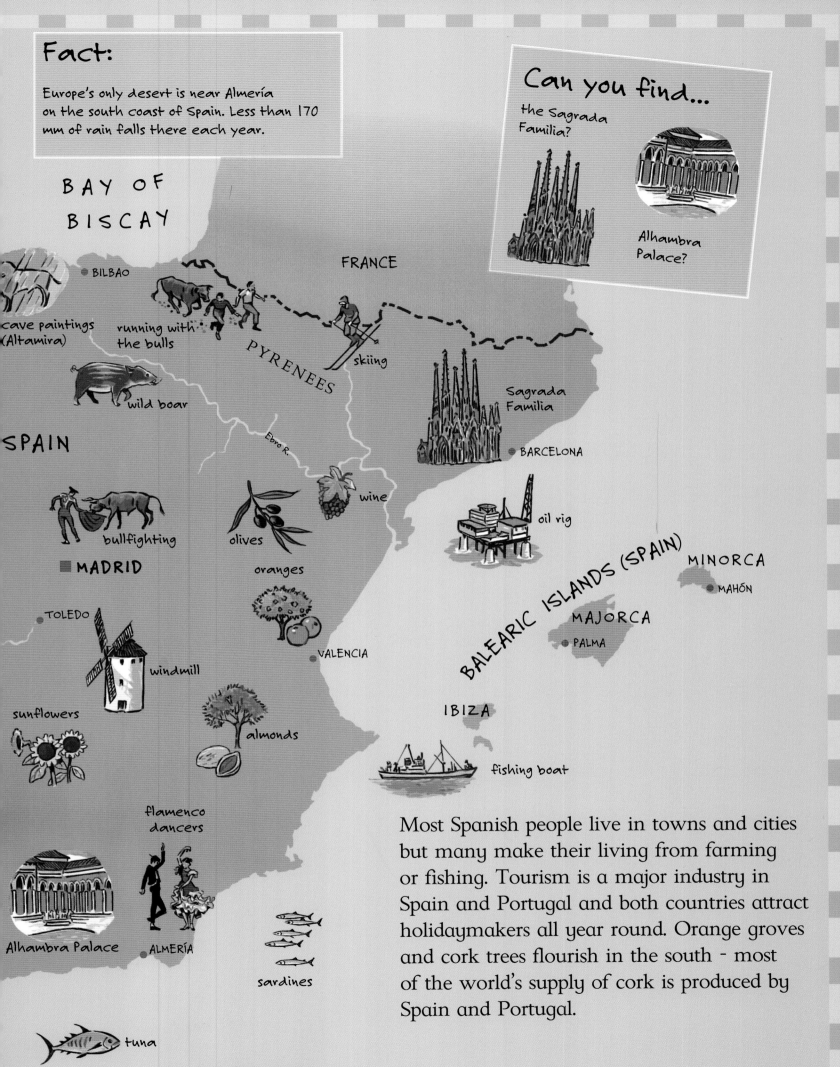

Fact:

Europe's only desert is near Almería on the south coast of Spain. Less than 170 mm of rain falls there each year.

Can you find...

the Sagrada Familia?

Alhambra Palace?

BAY OF BISCAY

FRANCE

BILBAO

cave paintings (Altamira)

running with the bulls

PYRENEES

skiing

wild boar

SPAIN

Ebro R.

Sagrada Familia

BARCELONA

bullfighting

olives

wine

MADRID

oranges

oil rig

BALEARIC ISLANDS (SPAIN)

MINORCA

MAHÓN

TOLEDO

windmill

VALENCIA

MAJORCA

PALMA

sunflowers

almonds

IBIZA

fishing boat

flamenco dancers

Most Spanish people live in towns and cities but many make their living from farming or fishing. Tourism is a major industry in Spain and Portugal and both countries attract holidaymakers all year round. Orange groves and cork trees flourish in the south - most of the world's supply of cork is produced by Spain and Portugal.

Alhambra Palace

ALMERÍA

sardines

tuna

MEDITERRANEAN SEA

27

France

France is one of Europe's largest farming and industrial countries. Its mild climate becomes hotter and drier towards its southern borders with Italy and Spain. France is famous for its fine food and wines.

Can you find...

the Eiffel Tower?

the amphitheatre at Arles?

Mont St. Michel?

Much of France is farmland but most people now live in towns and cities.

The area around Paris, the capital city, is densely populated. Paris is famous for its great fashion houses, its smart restaurants and as a centre for the arts.

Andorra and Monaco are small, independent countries. Many wealthy people choose to live in Monaco because of its tax laws.

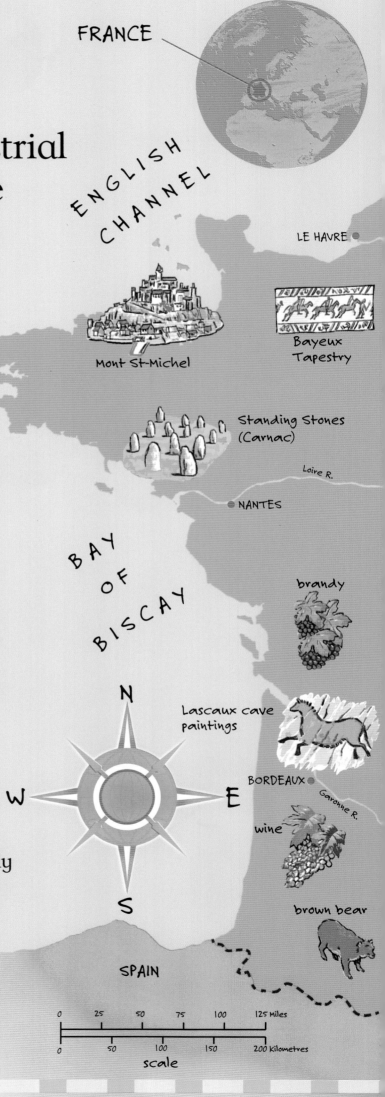

FRANCE

ENGLISH CHANNEL

LE HAVRE

Mont St-Michel

Bayeux Tapestry

Standing Stones (Carnac)

Loire R.

NANTES

BAY OF BISCAY

brandy

Lascaux cave paintings

N

W   E

S

BORDEAUX

Garonne R.

wine

brown bear

SPAIN

0   25   50   75   100   125 Miles

0   50   100   150   200 Kilometres

scale

Channel Tunnel

CALAIS

BELGIUM

LUXEMBOURG

When the Eiffel Tower was built in 1889, many Parisians thought it was an eyesore.
It is now the most famous landmark in France.

Eiffel Tower

Seine R.

PARIS

Marne R.

Seine R.

Chartres Cathedral

wine

wild boar

GERMANY

To ask someone their name in French you say, 'Comment t'appelles-tu?' (com-on-tap-el-to).

ALPS

mustard

deer

SWITZERLAND

FRANCE

TGV

LYON

Rhône R.

skiing

ALPS

ITALY

Fact:

The TGV is one of the world's fastest trains. It has a top speed of 320 kph.

Tour de France

amphitheatre

wine

chamois

MONTE CARLO
MONACO

TOULOUSE

ARLES

MEDITERRANEAN SEA

CORSICA (FRANCE)

AJACCIO

PYRENEES

ANDORRA LA VELLA
ANDORRA

Belgium, the Netherlands and Luxembourg

This part of Europe is called 'the Low Countries'. Most of the land in these countries is flat. Large areas of land have been reclaimed from the sea by draining it and building long dykes (walls) to protect the land from flooding.

N
W
S
E

BELGIUM, THE NETHERLANDS AND LUXEMBOURG

windmill

clogs

seal

ice skating

THE NETHERLANDS

GERMANY

AMSTERDAM
canal house

IJssel R.

Delft pottery

Edam cheese

diamond cutting

tulips

ROTTERDAM

Lek R.

Belgium is famous for lacemaking and fine chocolate.

THE HAGUE

NORTH SEA

Fact:

Windmills are common in the Netherlands.
They were used to pump water from the fields in the 18th and 19th centuries.

GERMANY

Maas R.

wheat

LUXEMBOURG

wine

LUXEMBOURG

wild boar

red deer

wild cat

Meuse R.

Amsterdam is a city of canals – there are more than 150 of them. Many people live on the canals in houseboats.

Antwerp Cathedral

Sambre R.

BRUSSELS

BELGIUM

Belgian chocolates

ANTWERP

GHENT

Scheldt R.

FRANCE

OSTEND

BRUGES

Bruges Town Hall

oysters

Can you find...

a windmill?

Antwerp Cathedral?

The Netherlands is famous for the cheese, flowers and bulbs it exports worldwide. Belgium produces steel and machinery. Luxembourg is a small but very wealthy nation and an important banking centre.

40 miles

0   25   50   75   100 kilometres

scale

0   30

31

Neuschwanstein Castle was built by King Ludwig of Bavaria. Walt Disney based his fairy-tale castle on this fantastic building.

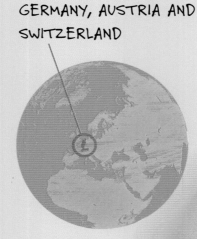

GERMANY, AUSTRIA AND SWITZERLAND

NORTH SEA

NETHERLANDS

Weser R.

Rhine R.

sausages

Cologne Cathedral

DÜSSELDORF

COLOGNE

BONN
Beethoven's birthplace

BELGIUM

LUXEMBOURG

Roman ruins

FRANCE

cuckoo clock

wine

watch-making

ZURICH

Gruyère cheese

■ BERN

SWITZERLAND

chocolates

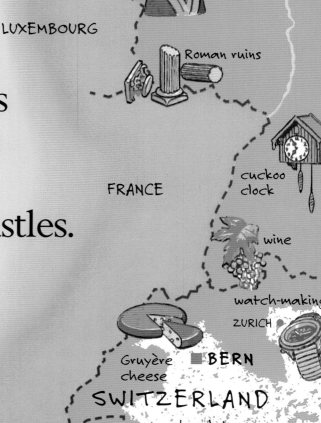

Germany, Austria and Switzerland

Germany is a wealthy industrial nation. It produces cars, electrical goods, wines and beers. It has a large population and many large cities. There are forests, long rivers and lots of fine castles. Germany's large rivers are important for transporting goods around the country.

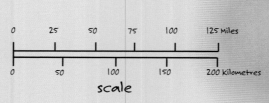

| 0 | 25 | 50 | 75 | 100 | 125 Miles |

| 0 | 50 | 100 | 150 | 200 Kilometres |

scale

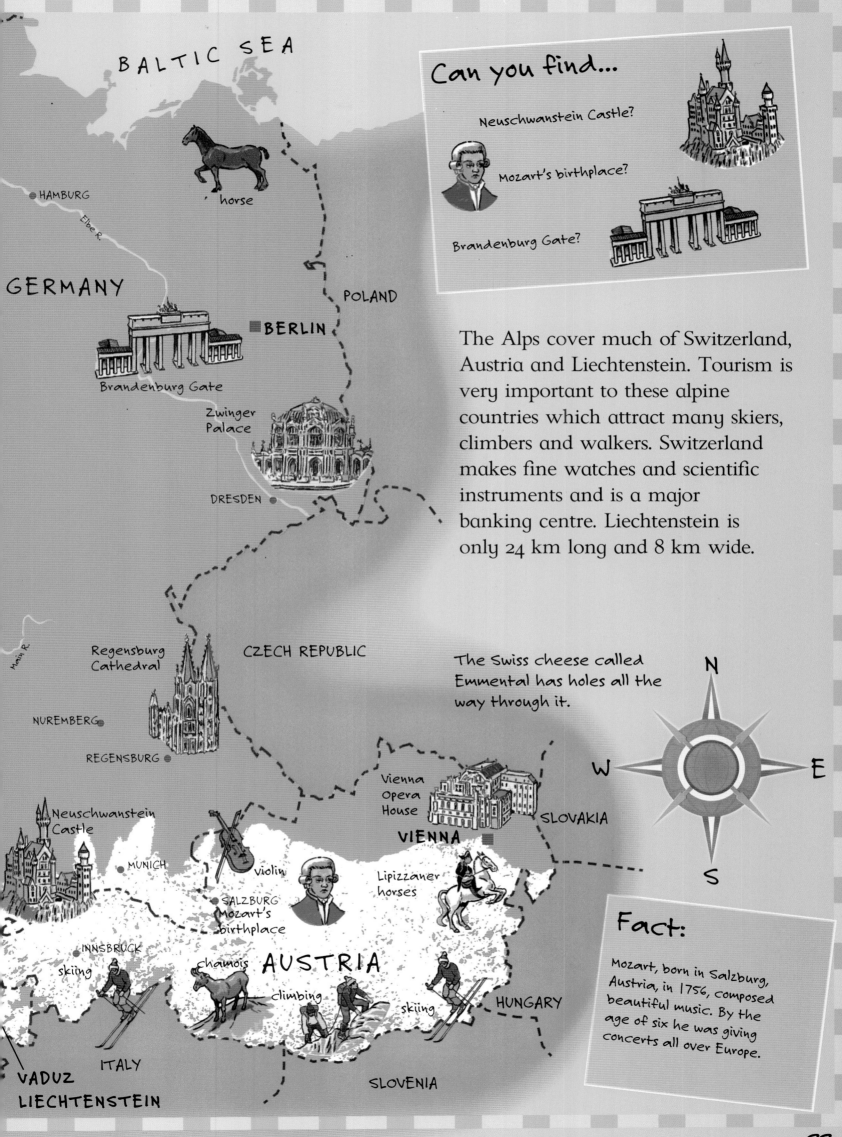

BALTIC SEA

HAMBURG

Elbe R.

horse

GERMANY

POLAND

Brandenburg Gate

BERLIN

Zwinger Palace

DRESDEN

Main R.

Regensburg Cathedral

CZECH REPUBLIC

NUREMBERG

REGENSBURG

Neuschwanstein Castle

MUNICH

violin

SALZBURG Mozart's birthplace

Vienna Opera House

VIENNA

SLOVAKIA

Lipizzaner horses

INNSBRUCK

skiing

chamois

AUSTRIA

climbing

skiing

HUNGARY

VADUZ

ITALY

SLOVENIA

LIECHTENSTEIN

Can you find...

Neuschwanstein Castle?

Mozart's birthplace?

Brandenburg Gate?

The Alps cover much of Switzerland, Austria and Liechtenstein. Tourism is very important to these alpine countries which attract many skiers, climbers and walkers. Switzerland makes fine watches and scientific instruments and is a major banking centre. Liechtenstein is only 24 km long and 8 km wide.

The Swiss cheese called Emmental has holes all the way through it.

N
W   E
S

Fact:

Mozart, born in Salzburg, Austria, in 1756, composed beautiful music. By the age of six he was giving concerts all over Europe.

Italy and Malta

Italy is famous for its art, food, fashion and cars. Most of its population, industry and farmland are concentrated along the River Po in the north.

Can you find...

Pompeii?

the Leaning Tower of Pisa?

the Colosseum?

Fact:

Pizza is a traditional food that was invented in Italy. It is now eaten worldwide.

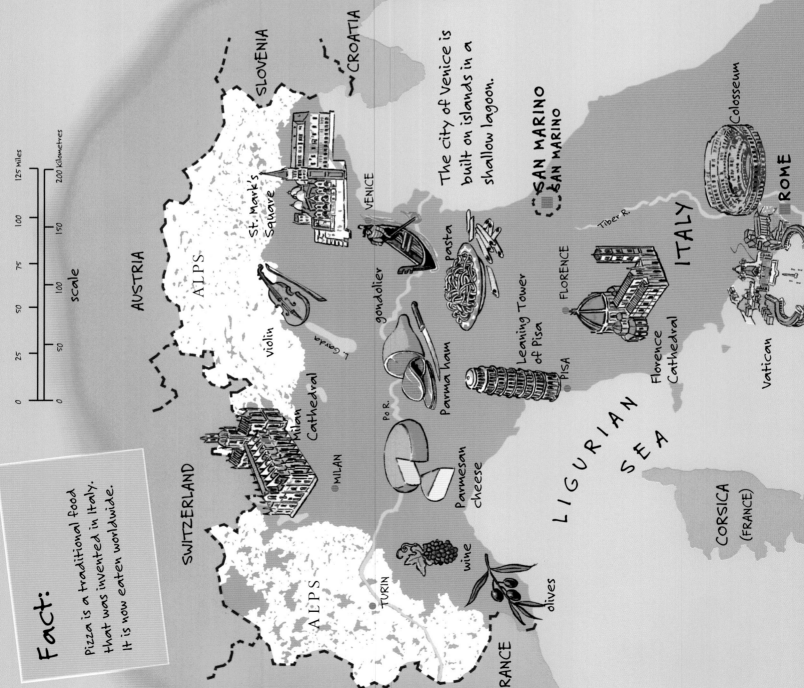

scale

0	25	50	75	100		125 miles
0	50	100	150	200 Kilometres		

SWITZERLAND

FRANCE

ALPS

AUSTRIA

ALPS

SLOVENIA

CROATIA

St. Mark's Square

VENICE

The city of Venice is built on islands in a shallow lagoon.

violin

Milan Cathedral

MILAN

Parmesan cheese

L. Garda

Po R.

gondolier

Parma ham

pasta

SAN MARINO
SAN MARINO

TURIN

wine

olives

Leaning Tower of Pisa

PISA

FLORENCE

Florence Cathedral

Tiber R.

ITALY

ROME

Colosseum

Vatican

VATICAN CITY

CORSICA (FRANCE)

LIGURIAN SEA

ADRIATIC SEA

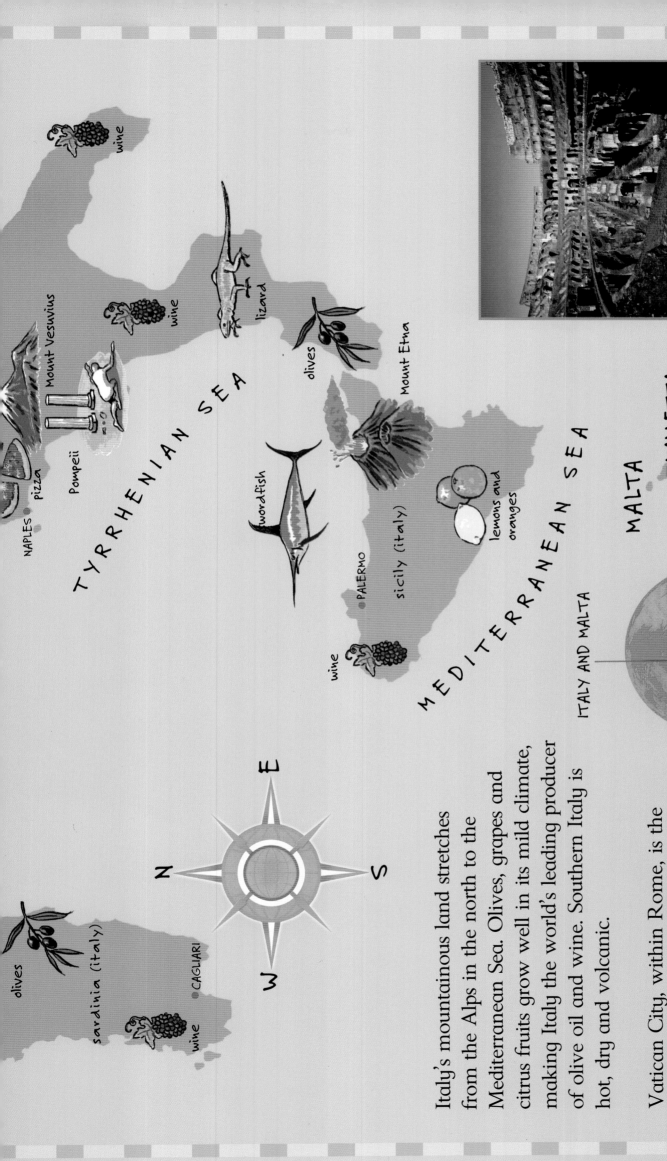

wine

wine

Mount Vesuvius

Pompeii

pizza

NAPLES

olives

wine

lizard

TYRRHENIAN SEA

olives

Mount Etna

swordfish

PALERMO

sicily (italy)

wine

lemons and oranges

MEDITERRANEAN SEA

MALTA

VALLETTA

olives

sardinia (italy)

wine CAGLIARI

N
E
W
S

ITALY AND MALTA

Italy's mountainous land stretches from the Alps in the north to the Mediterranean Sea. Olives, grapes and citrus fruits grow well in its mild climate, making Italy the world's leading producer of olive oil and wine. Southern Italy is hot, dry and volcanic.

Vatican City, within Rome, is the world's smallest state. It is home to the Pope, the head of the Roman Catholic Church. Vatican City has its own government, newspaper, coins, stamps and radio station.

Italy was the centre of the ancient Roman Empire. Today, buildings such as the Roman Colosseum attract thousands of tourists.

Malta depends on income from tourism and its shipping ports.

GREECE AND THE
GREEK ISLANDS

N

W E

S

scale

0   25   50   75   100 miles

0 50 100 150 kilometres

Can you find...

King Agamemnon's mask?

the Acropolis?

Octopus and calamari (squid) are popular foods in Greece.

TURKEY

BULGARIA

MACEDONIA

ALBANIA

THESSALONIKI

AEGEAN SEA

LIMNOS

LESVOS

CHIOS

IKARIA

SAMOS

SKIATHOS

SKYROS

EVVOIA

ATHENS

Acropolis

parliament guard

GREECE

goat

olives

sheep

balalaika

CORFU

PATRAS

wine

CEPHALONIA

ZAKYNTHOS

IONIAN SEA

36

Greece and the Greek Islands

Greece is in southern Europe. It is a dry, mountainous country with many islands. The capital city, Athens, is home to more than one third of Greece's population. Farming and tourism are the major industries.

The Ancient Greeks were Europe's first great civilisation. Each year, thousands of tourists explore Greece's ancient buildings and archaeological sites. Greece is a popular holiday destination, attracting many visitors with its scenery, sunshine and fine beaches. Its hot climate is ideal for growing olives, grapes and citrus fruits.

The Parthenon is an ancient Greek temple. It stands on the Acropolis - a rocky hill that towers over the city of Athens.

Fact:

Ancient Greece was the birthplace of democracy.

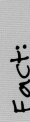

King Agamemnon's mask

olives

octopus

THIRA

NAXOS

KOS

RHODES

MEDITERRANEAN SEA

dolphins

● IRAKLION

CRETE

olives

wine

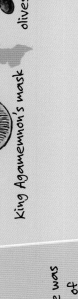

The south of the region is rugged and mountainous with many areas of rich farmland. In 1993 Czechoslovakia split into two countries: the Czech Republic and Slovakia. Slovenia, Bosnia and Herzegovina, Croatia, and Macedonia were all once part of Yugoslavia, but have recently become independent countries.

Hungarian goulash is a dish made from beef, spicy pepper and sour cream.

150 miles

200 kilometres

scale

N
E
W
S

Can you find...

Alexander Nevsky Cathedral

Bratislava Castle

CENTRAL AND EASTERN EUROPE

BALTIC SEA

RUSSIA

LITHUANIA

BELARUS

UKRAINE

European bison

WARSAW

POLAND

CRACOW

skiing

brown bear

windmill

GERMANY

PRAGUE
CZECH REPUBLIC

SLOVAKIA

Bratislava Castle

BRATISLAVA

R. Danube

HUNGARY

Budapest Parliament

wild cat

AUSTRIA

SLOVENIA

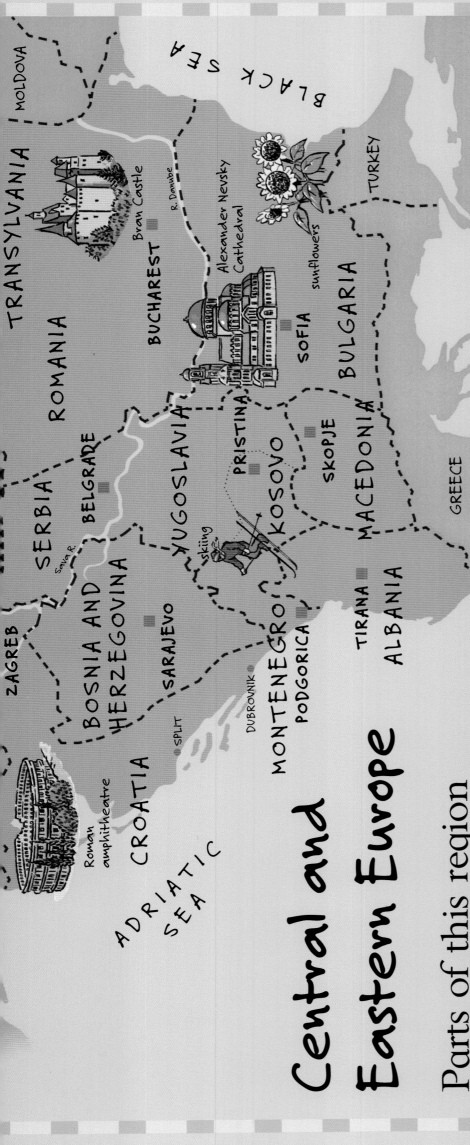

MOLDOVA

TRANSYLVANIA

BLACK SEA

Bran Castle

R. Danube

Alexander Nevsky Cathedral

TURKEY

BUCHAREST

ROMANIA

sunflowers

SOFIA

BULGARIA

SERBIA

BELGRADE

Sava R.

ZAGREB

BOSNIA AND HERZEGOVINA

SARAJEVO

YUGOSLAVIA

PRISTINA

KOSOVO

SKOPJE

MACEDONIA

skiing

GREECE

MONTENEGRO

PODGORICA

DUBROVNIK

TIRANA

ALBANIA

SPLIT

Roman amphitheatre

CROATIA

ADRIATIC SEA

Central and Eastern Europe

Parts of this region suffered bitter fighting during the 1990s. Borders were redrawn and new countries have been created. Poland, the largest and most populated country in the region, has major iron, steel and shipbuilding industries.

Facts:

- Heavy industry has caused serious pollution problems in Poland, Hungary and the Czech Republic.

- Budapest, the capital city of Hungary, was once two towns separated by the River Danube. One town was called Buda and the other Pest.

Northern Eurasia

This vast region stretches across Asia and Europe. Until 1991 it was one single country, the Soviet Union. Today, it is made up of 15 independent nations including Russia, the largest country in the world.

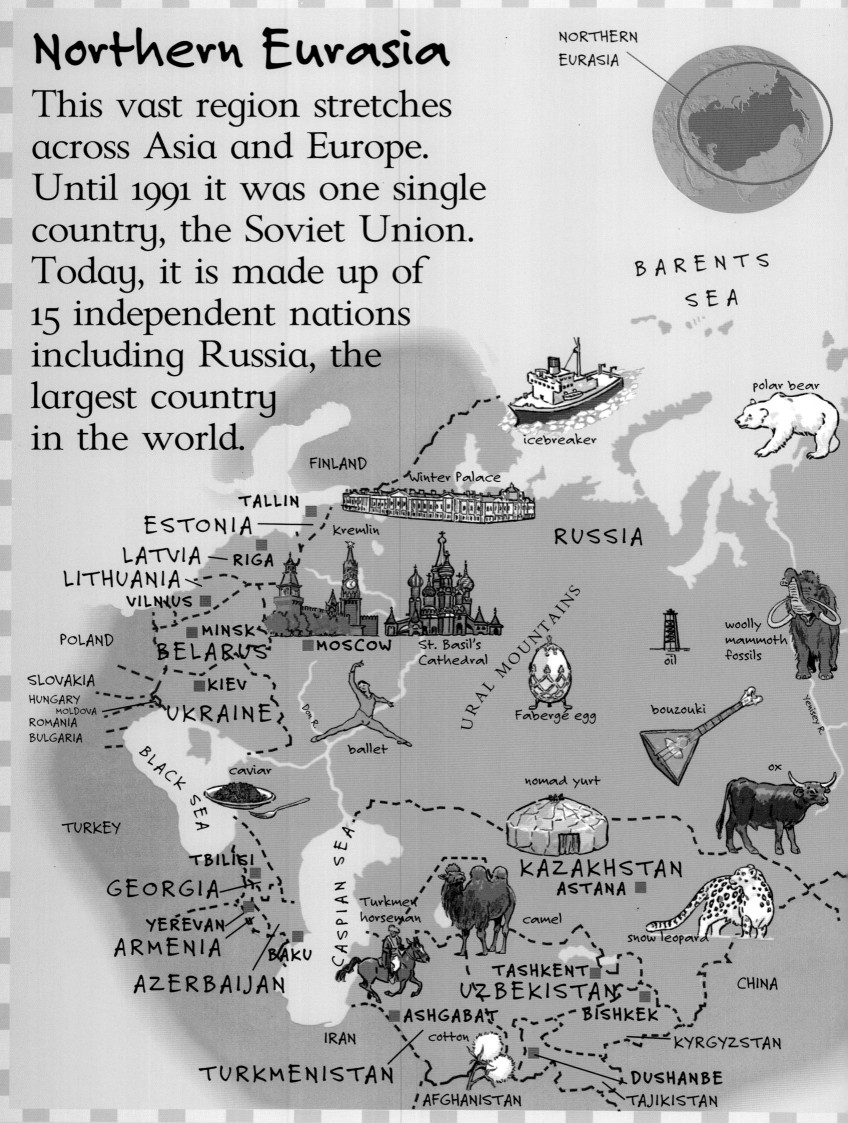

NORTHERN EURASIA

BARENTS SEA

polar bear

icebreaker

FINLAND

Winter Palace

RUSSIA

TALLIN

ESTONIA

Kremlin

LATVIA — RIGA

LITHUANIA

VILNIUS

POLAND

MINSK

BELARUS

MOSCOW

St. Basil's Cathedral

URAL MOUNTAINS

oil

woolly mammoth fossils

Yenisey R.

SLOVAKIA

HUNGARY

MOLDOVA

ROMANIA

BULGARIA

KIEV

UKRAINE

Don R.

ballet

Fabergé egg

bouzouki

ox

BLACK SEA

caviar

nomad yurt

TURKEY

snow leopard

TBILISI

GEORGIA

CASPIAN SEA

Turkmen horseman

KAZAKHSTAN

ASTANA

camel

YEREVAN

ARMENIA

BAKU

AZERBAIJAN

TASHKENT

UZBEKISTAN

CHINA

ASHGABAT

BISHKEK

IRAN

cotton

KYRGYZSTAN

TURKMENISTAN

DUSHANBE

AFGHANISTAN

TAJIKISTAN

Vast forests and grasslands separate the Arctic land in the north from the deserts which cover most of Kazakhstan, Uzbekistan and Turkmenistan in the south. Most of Russia's population, industry and fertile land are west of the Ural Mountains. To the east, Siberia is rich in oil and coal but few people live there as the climate is bitterly cold.

ARCTIC OCEAN

polar bear

wolf

lynx

Opala volcano

SIBERIA

Lena R.

elk

brown bear

gold

Lower Tunguska R.

SEA OF OKHOTSK

PACIFIC OCEAN

Manchurian tiger

wheat

Trans-Siberian Railway

L. Baikal

CHINA

VLADIVOSTOK

MONGOLIA

St. Basil's Cathedral was built in 1555 by Ivan the Terrible. It stands next to Red Square in the centre of Moscow.

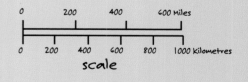

0	200	400	600 Miles

0	200	400	600	800	1000 Kilometres

scale

Fact:

Siberia is a vast wilderness. It is one of the world's coldest places. A temperature as low as -71°C has been recorded there.

It takes eight days to travel the length of the Trans-Siberian Railway line from Moscow to Vladivostok (9,297 km).

N

E

W

S

Can you find...

the Royal Tomb at Petra?

the Suleymaniye Mosque?

SOUTHWEST ASIA

BULGARIA

GREECE

BLACK SE

ISTANBUL

TURKEY
■ ANKARA

Suleymaniye Mosque

whirling dervish

Krak des Chevaliers

MEDITERRANEAN SEA

TURKISH STATE OF CYPRUS

NICOSIA ■

CYPRUS

BEIRUT

LEBANON

SYRIA

WEST BANK (disputed)

DAMASCUS

JERUSALEM ■

■ AMMAN

JORDAN

Dome of the Rock

ISRAEL

Dead Sea

EGYPT

Petra

scorpion

MECCA

JEDDAH

RED SEA

Southwest Asia

This area, also known as the Middle East, is mainly hot and dry with vast arid deserts to the south. It is a huge oil-producing region, supplying much of the world's oil.

The Middle East has long been troubled by wars between neighbouring countries. The discovery of large amounts of oil and natural gas around the Persian Gulf has brought great wealth to the region.

Fact:

The Dead Sea lies on the border of Israel and Jordan. Its water is so salty that people can float in it without swimming – it is impossible to sink.

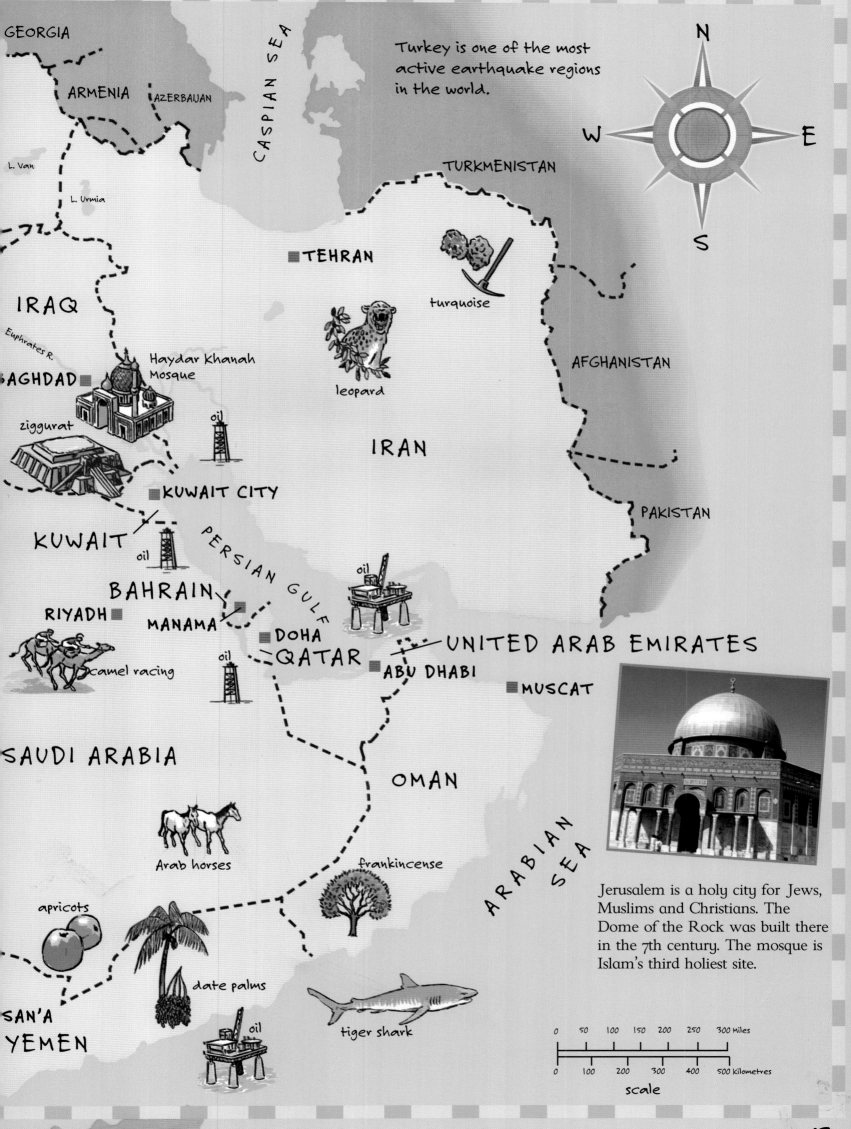

GEORGIA

ARMENIA

AZERBAIJAN

CASPIAN SEA

Turkey is one of the most active earthquake regions in the world.

N
W   E
S

L. Van

L. Urmia

TURKMENISTAN

IRAQ

Euphrates R.

TEHRAN

turquoise

leopard

AFGHANISTAN

BAGHDAD

Haydar Khanah Mosque

ziggurat

oil

IRAN

KUWAIT CITY

PAKISTAN

KUWAIT

oil

PERSIAN GULF

oil

BAHRAIN

RIYADH

MANAMA

DOHA

QATAR

UNITED ARAB EMIRATES

ABU DHABI

MUSCAT

camel racing

oil

SAUDI ARABIA

OMAN

Arab horses

frankincense

ARABIAN SEA

Jerusalem is a holy city for Jews, Muslims and Christians. The Dome of the Rock was built there in the 7th century. The mosque is Islam's third holiest site.

apricots

date palms

oil

SAN'A

YEMEN

tiger shark

scale

0 50 100 150 200 250 300 Miles

0 100 200 300 400 500 Kilometres

43

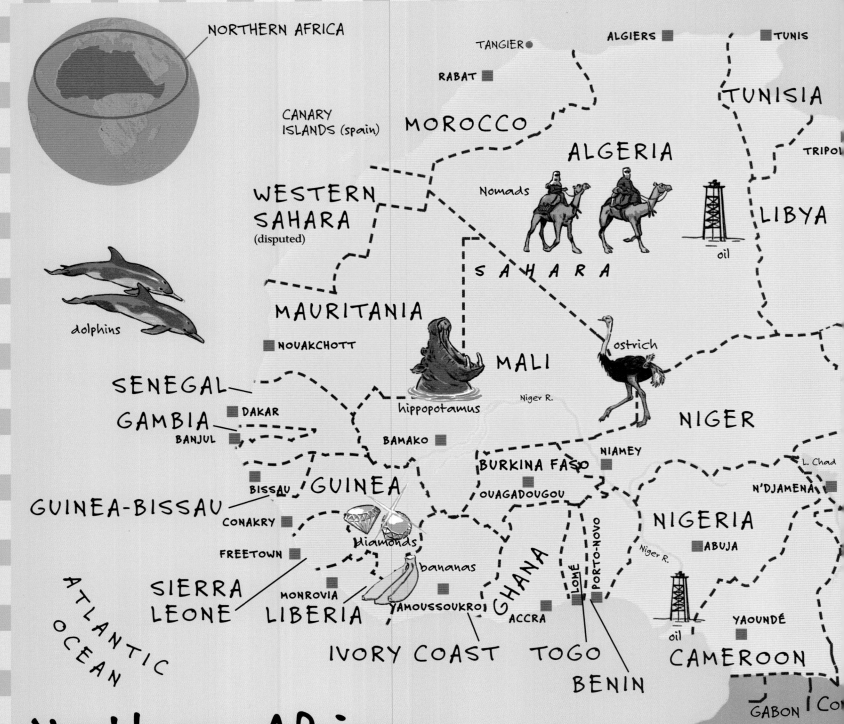

NORTHERN AFRICA

TANGIER ○
ALGIERS ■   ■ TUNIS
RABAT ■
CANARY
ISLANDS (spain)   MOROCCO   TUNISIA
                                  ALGERIA   TRIPOL■
WESTERN
SAHARA   Nomads   LIBYA
(disputed)

                    S A H A R A   oil

dolphins

MAURITANIA
■ NOUAKCHOTT   MALI   ostrich

SENEGAL   DAKAR   Niger R.   NIGER
GAMBIA ■
BANJUL ■   BAMAKO ■
                                  NIAMEY   L. Chad
                    BURKINA FASO ■
BISSAU ■ GUINEA   OUAGADOUGOU ■   N'DJAMENA ■
GUINEA-BISSAU   diamonds   NIGERIA
CONAKRY ■   Niger R. ■ ABUJA
FREETOWN ■   bananas   PORTO-NOVO
                                  GHANA LOMÉ   oil
SIERRA   MONROVIA ■   YAMOUSSOUKRO   YAOUNDÉ ■
LEONE   LIBERIA   ACCRA   oil CAMEROON
ATLANTIC
OCEAN   IVORY COAST TOGO
                              BENIN
                                        GABON | Co

Northern Africa

Much of the huge continent of Africa is hot and dry. The land along the Mediterranean coast and the Nile Valley is rich and fertile. The vast Sahara Desert covers more than half of north Africa.

Facts:

- The Sahara Desert is the largest desert in the world, covering about 9,000,000 square kilometres.
- Nigeria's oil industry makes it one of the richest countries in Africa.

The Nile Valley in Egypt is the most densely populated region. Lagos in Nigeria is Africa's largest city.

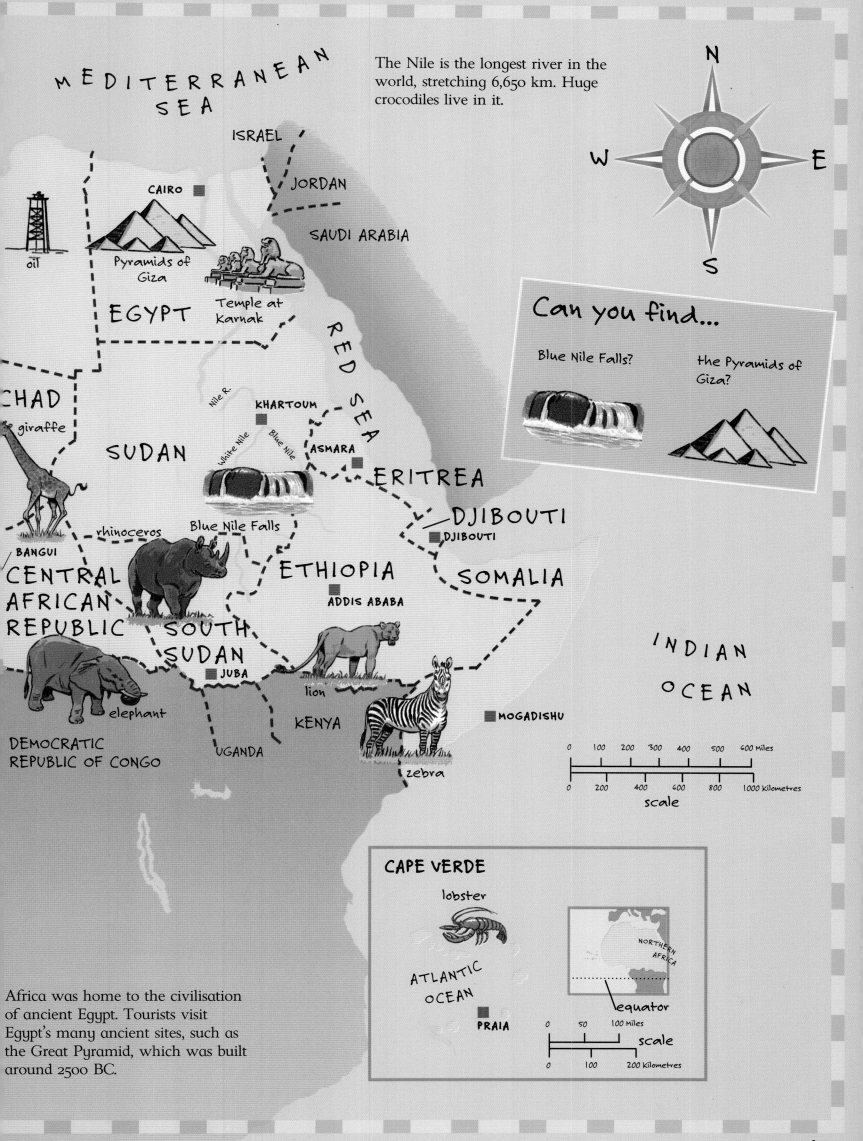

MEDITERRANEAN SEA

The Nile is the longest river in the world, stretching 6,650 km. Huge crocodiles live in it.

ISRAEL

JORDAN

SAUDI ARABIA

CAIRO

oil

Pyramids of Giza

Temple at Karnak

EGYPT

RED SEA

Nile R.

KHARTOUM

White Nile

Blue Nile

ASMARA

ERITREA

DJIBOUTI

DJIBOUTI

SUDAN

giraffe

rhinoceros

Blue Nile Falls

BANGUI

CENTRAL AFRICAN REPUBLIC

SOUTH SUDAN

ETHIOPIA

ADDIS ABABA

SOMALIA

JUBA

lion

elephant

KENYA

zebra

MOGADISHU

DEMOCRATIC REPUBLIC OF CONGO

UGANDA

INDIAN OCEAN

Can you find...

Blue Nile Falls?

the Pyramids of Giza?

| 0 | 100 | 200 | 300 | 400 | 500 | 600 Miles |

| 0 | 200 | 400 | 600 | 800 | 1000 Kilometres |

scale

Africa was home to the civilisation of ancient Egypt. Tourists visit Egypt's many ancient sites, such as the Great Pyramid, which was built around 2500 BC.

CAPE VERDE

lobster

ATLANTIC OCEAN

NORTHERN AFRICA

equator

PRAIA

| 0 | 50 | 100 Miles |

scale

| 0 | 100 | 200 Kilometres |

45

pygmies

MALABO ☐ CAMEROON

EQUATORIAL GUINEA

chimpanzee
☐ LIBREVILLE

GABON

rainforest

CONGO REPUBLIC — BRAZZAVILLE

flying fish

KINSHASA

CABINDA (ANGOLA)

☐ LUANDA

ANGOLA

Southern Africa

The mighty Congo River runs through dense, tropical rainforests in Central Africa. Crocodiles, chimpanzees and gorillas live in these hot, steamy forests. Grasslands and deserts make up much of Southern Africa, but there is rich farmland in the far south.

ATLANTIC OCEAN

diamonds

oil

springbok

meerkats

NAMIBIA

WINDHOEK

diamonds

SOUTH AFRICA

wine

CAPE TOWN

Can you find...

Victoria Falls?

meerkats?

Fact:

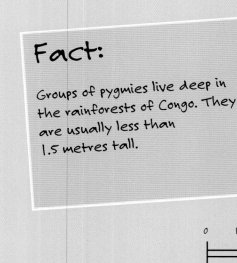

Groups of pygmies live deep in the rainforests of Congo. They are usually less than 1.5 metres tall.

scale

0	100	200	300	400	500	600 Miles

0	200	400	600	800	1000 Kilometres

SOUTH SUDAN

ETHIOPIA

EMOCRATIC
EPUBLIC OF
ONGO

Congo (Zaire) R.

Ankole
cattle

SOMALIA

UGANDA

KENYA

KAMPALA

NAIROBI

KIGALI

L. Victoria

RWANDA

Mt. Kilimanjaro

BUJUMBURA

cheetah

BURUNDI

TANZANIA

ZANZIBAR

L. Tanganyika

great white shark

SOUTHERN AFRICA

The top of Mount Kilimanjaro in Tanzania is covered in snow all year round.

bananas

DAR ES
SALAAM

giraffe

cashew nuts

SEYCHELLES

VICTORIA

elephant

COMOROS

ZAMBIA

MALAWI

MORONI

LUSAKA

LILONGWE

Victoria
Falls

L. Nyasa

coconuts

Zambezi R.

aardvark

HARARE

MOZAMBIQUE

ANTANANARIVO

ZIMBABWE

MADAGASCAR

MAURITIUS

TSWANA

Cape buffalo

SAINT-DENIS

Orange R.

rugby

PORT
LOUIS

RÉUNION

ABORONE

MAPUTO

chameleon

RETORIA

MBABANE

SWAZILAND

gold

MASERU

LESOTHO

BLOEMFONTEIN

INDIAN OCEAN

Africa is the world's second largest continent and is made up of many countries. South Africa is rich in copper, gold and diamonds. It is also an important farming region. Large nature reserves have been created all over Southern Africa to protect some of its wild animals. The land is home to zebras, lions, cheetahs, leopards, elephants, rhinoceroses, ostriches and giraffes.

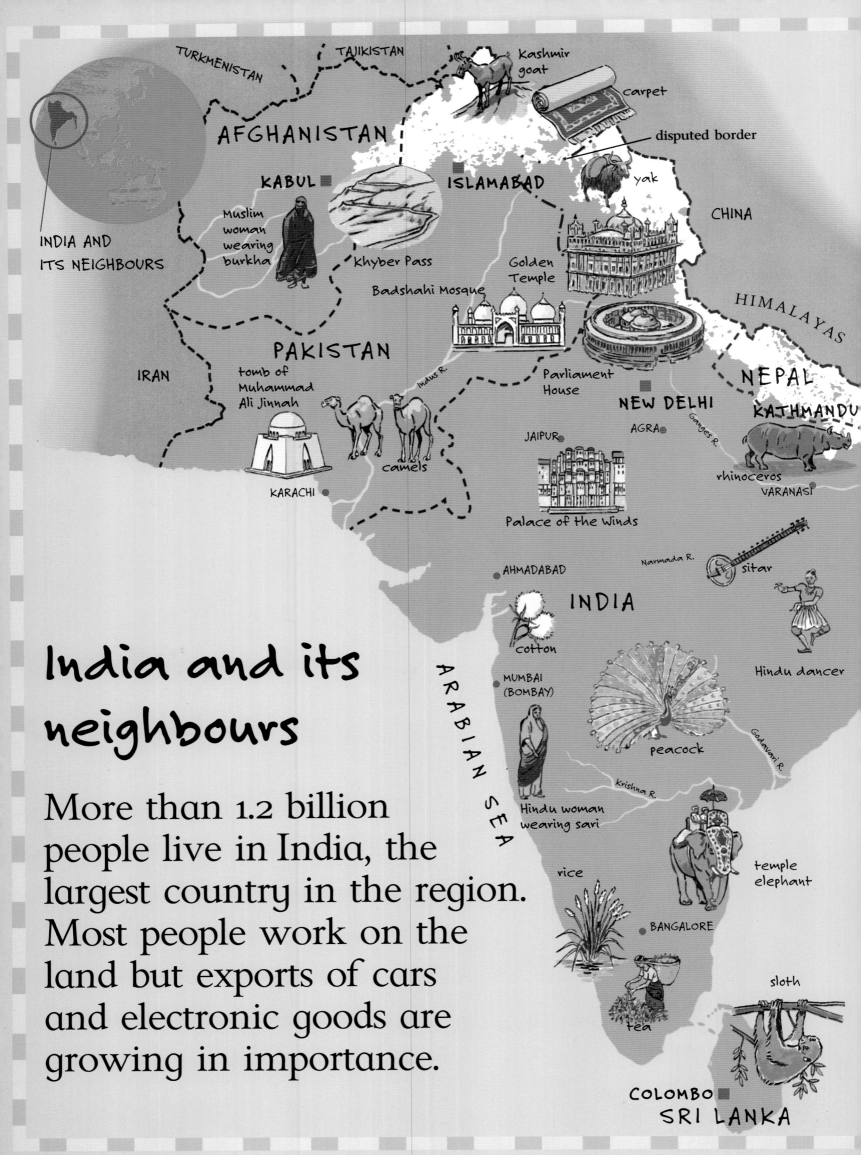

India and its neighbours

More than 1.2 billion people live in India, the largest country in the region. Most people work on the land but exports of cars and electronic goods are growing in importance.

INDIA AND ITS NEIGHBOURS

TURKMENISTAN
TAJIKISTAN
Kashmir goat
carpet
disputed border

AFGHANISTAN
KABUL
ISLAMABAD
yak
CHINA

Muslim woman wearing burkha
Khyber Pass
Golden Temple
Badshahi Mosque
HIMALAYAS

PAKISTAN
IRAN
tomb of Muhammad Ali Jinnah
Indus R.
Parliament House
NEPAL
KATHMANDU

camels
NEW DELHI
JAIPUR
AGRA
Ganges R.
rhinoceros
VARANASI

KARACHI
Palace of the Winds

AHMADABAD
Narmada R.
sitar

INDIA
cotton
Hindu dancer

ARABIAN SEA
MUMBAI (BOMBAY)
peacock
Godavari R.

Hindu woman wearing sari
Krishna R.

rice
temple elephant

BANGALORE

tea
sloth

COLOMBO
SRI LANKA

48

Can you find...

the Palace of the Winds?

the Golden Temple?

a temple elephant?

Vast mountain ranges separate this region from Central Asia. The climate is hot and dry, so many people live on the coast or on the fertile plains along the Ganges and Indus rivers. India, Bangladesh and Sri Lanka are some of the world's main tea-growing nations. Most industries are concentrated in the large crowded cities of India and Pakistan.

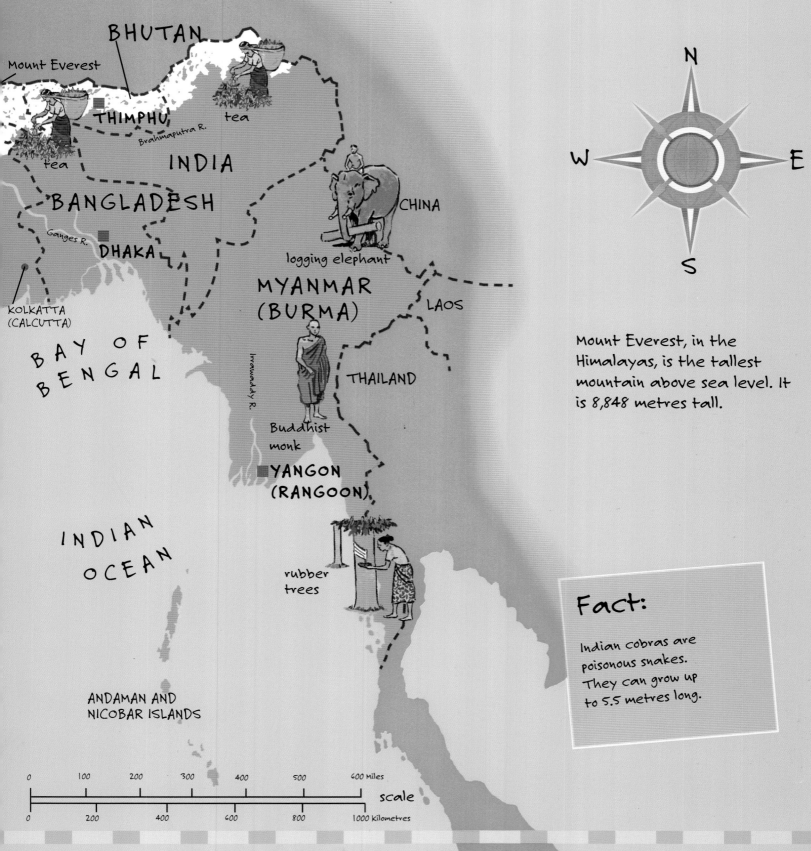

BHUTAN

Mount Everest

THIMPHU

tea

Brahmaputra R.

INDIA

tea

BANGLADESH

Ganges R.

DHAKA

KOLKATTA (CALCUTTA)

BAY OF BENGAL

CHINA

logging elephant

MYANMAR (BURMA)

LAOS

Irrawaddy R.

THAILAND

Buddhist monk

YANGON (RANGOON)

INDIAN OCEAN

rubber trees

ANDAMAN AND NICOBAR ISLANDS

N

W   E

S

Mount Everest, in the Himalayas, is the tallest mountain above sea level. It is 8,848 metres tall.

Fact:

Indian cobras are poisonous snakes. They can grow up to 5.5 metres long.

| 0 | 100 | 200 | 300 | 400 | 500 | 600 Miles |

scale

| 0 | 200 | 400 | 600 | 800 | 1000 Kilometres |

Japan

Japan is made up of four large islands and thousands of smaller ones. It lies off the east coast of China. Japan's cities are built along its flat coastland because mountains and forests cover much of the country inland.

About 38 million people live in and around Tokyo, Japan's capital city.

N
W E
S

JAPAN

mako shark

RYUKYU ISLANDS (Japan)

karate

NAHA

EAST CHINA SEA

CHINA

JAPAN

scale (Ryukyu Islands)

0   50   100 miles
0   100   200 kilometres

brown bear

hokkaidō

paper making

SHIKARI

SAPPORO

bonsai tree

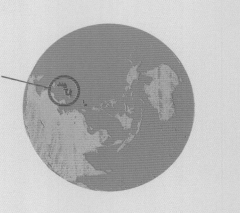

tea ceremony

JAPANESE ALPS

SENDAI

Honshū

women's traditional costume

oysters

10 R.

Can you find...

Mt. Fuji?

Osaka Castle?

Torii Gate?

YOKOHAMA

Mount Fuji

JAPAN

L. Biwa

KYOTO

KOBE • OSAKA

Osaka Castle

SEA OF JAPAN (EAST SEA)

Temple of the Golden Pavilion

chopsticks

• HIROSHIMA

shikoku

Torii Gate

kyūshū

kendo

• KAGOSHIMA

swordfish

Pearls

PACIFIC OCEAN

octopus

scale

0   25   50   75   100 miles

0   50   100   150 kilometres

Japan is a major industrial nation. It is famous for cars and cameras and exports many electrical goods. It is one of the richest countries in Asia. Northern Japan is cold but the southern climate is tropical. Earthquakes are common in Japan and the country is often hit by fierce storms called typhoons.

Mount Fuji is the highest volcano in Japan, reaching 3,776 metres at its summit. According to legend, an earthquake created Mount Fuji in 286 BC. Its last big eruption was in 1707.

Southeast Asia

Southeast Asia is made up of two small areas of mainland and almost 20,000 islands. The climate is hot and humid. Tropical rainforests cover much of this mountainous region and provide the world with most of its hardwoods.

Can you find...

Angkor Wat temple?

the skyscrapers of Singapore?

N
W   E
S

CHINA

elephant

VIETNAM

HANOI

MYANMAR (BURMA)

LAOS

VIENTIANE

folk dancer

THAILAND

BANGKOK

Angkor Wat

CAMBODIA

A N D A M A N   S E A

PHNOM PENH

HO CHI MINH CITY

rubber tree

leather back turtle

MALAYSIA

KUALA LUMPUR

tiger

SINGAPORE

SUMATRA

tea

I N D I A N   O C E A N

JAKARTA

JAVA

| 0 | 100 | 200 | 300 | 400 | 500 | 600 Miles |

| 0 | 200 | 400 | 600 | 800 | 1000 kilometres |

scale

SOUTHEAST ASIA

tiger shark

swordfish

■ MANILA

PHILIPPINES

In remote areas of Southeast Asia, people live in houses raised on stilts to avoid being flooded during the rainy season. Monsoon rains fall from June to October. The climate is ideal for growing rice, Southeast Asia's main crop. Pineapples, bananas, mangoes and coconuts are also grown.
The rainforests are rich in plantlife and are home to orang-utans, rhinoceroses, leopards and tigers.

pineapple

MINDANAO

BRUNEI
BANDAR-
SERI
BEGAWAN
MALAYSIA

Oil-rich Brunei is one of the world's smallest and wealthiest countries.

Hunter with blowpipe

PACIFIC OCEAN

BORNEO

coconuts

SULAWESI

rice

oil rig

house on stilts

coffee

IRIAN JAYA

PAPUA NEW GUINEA

INDONESIA

Borobudur Temple

EAST TIMOR

shadow puppet

Komodo dragon

hammerhead shark

AUSTRALIA

53

China, Mongolia, Korea and Taiwan

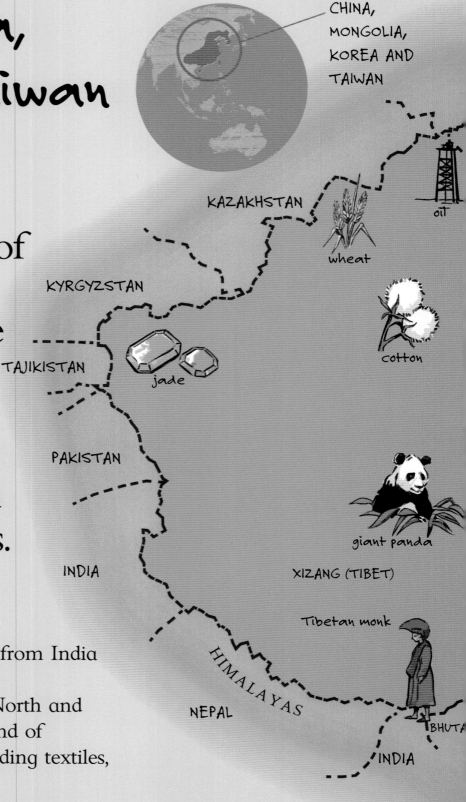

CHINA, MONGOLIA, KOREA AND TAIWAN

More people live in China than in any other country. Most of the population farm the fertile land in the east, growing rice, wheat, maize and tea. China is also an industrial nation and has many large cities.

High mountain ranges separate China from India and there are vast deserts to the north. The Korean peninsula is divided into North and South Korea. South Korea and the island of Taiwan have successful industries including textiles, cars and electrical goods.

KAZAKHSTAN

oil

wheat

KYRGYZSTAN

cotton

TAJIKISTAN

jade

PAKISTAN

giant panda

INDIA

XIZANG (TIBET)

Tibetan monk

HIMALAYAS

NEPAL

BHUTA

INDIA

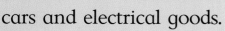

The Great Wall of China is 3,460 km long. But it's not true that you can see it from the Moon.

Can you find...

the Forbidden City?

the Potala Palace?

YAK

RUSSIA

sheep

Us L.

Selenge R.

elk

Hulun L.

tiger

Kerulen R.

MONGOLIA

ULAN BATOR

camel train

Temple of Heaven

NORTH KOREA

PYONGYANG

SEOUL

SOUTH KOREA

space rocket launch site

Great Wall of China

BEIJING

Forbidden City

CHINA

QINGDAO

Yellow R.

wheat

ZHENGZHOU

XI'AN

Terracotta Army

SHANGHAI

Potala Palace

SA

tea

Yangtze R.

Yangtze R.

fishing

pagoda

chopsticks

skyscrapers

XIAMEN

TAIPEI

TAIWAN

hi-tech goods

Xi R.

HONG KONG

rubber tree

MAR (BURMA)

VIETNAM

LAOS

hainan (china)

SOUTH CHINA SEA

junks

Fact:

More cars are made in China than in any other country.

AUSTRALIA AND PAPUA NEW GUINEA

Papua New Guinea has over 700 languages - more than any other country.

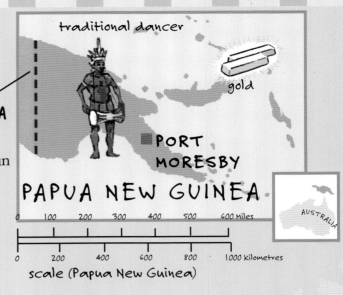

traditional dancer

IRIAN JAYA

gold

PORT MORESBY

PAPUA NEW GUINEA

AUSTRALIA

0   100   200   300   400   500   600 Miles

0   200   400   600   800   1000 Kilometres

scale (Papua New Guinea)

Australia and Papua New Guinea

Australia is the world's smallest continent. It is a wealthy country with a small population. It is hot and dry inland, so most people live in large coastal cities. Much of Australia's wealth comes from farming, mining and tourism.

Central Australia is called the 'outback'. It is mainly deserts and grasslands.
Few people live there, but vast numbers of sheep and cattle graze on stations (large farms). Australia produces more wool than any other country. It also has large deposits of opals, diamonds, gold and silver.

INDIAN OCEAN

pearls

baobab tree

emu

WESTERN AUSTRALIA

red kangaroo

dingo

cricket

gold

PERTH

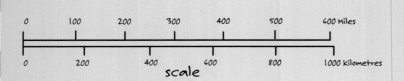

0   100   200   300   400   500   600 Miles

0   200   400   600   800   1000 Kilometres

scale

Can you find...

Sydney Opera House?

Ayers Rock (Uluru)?

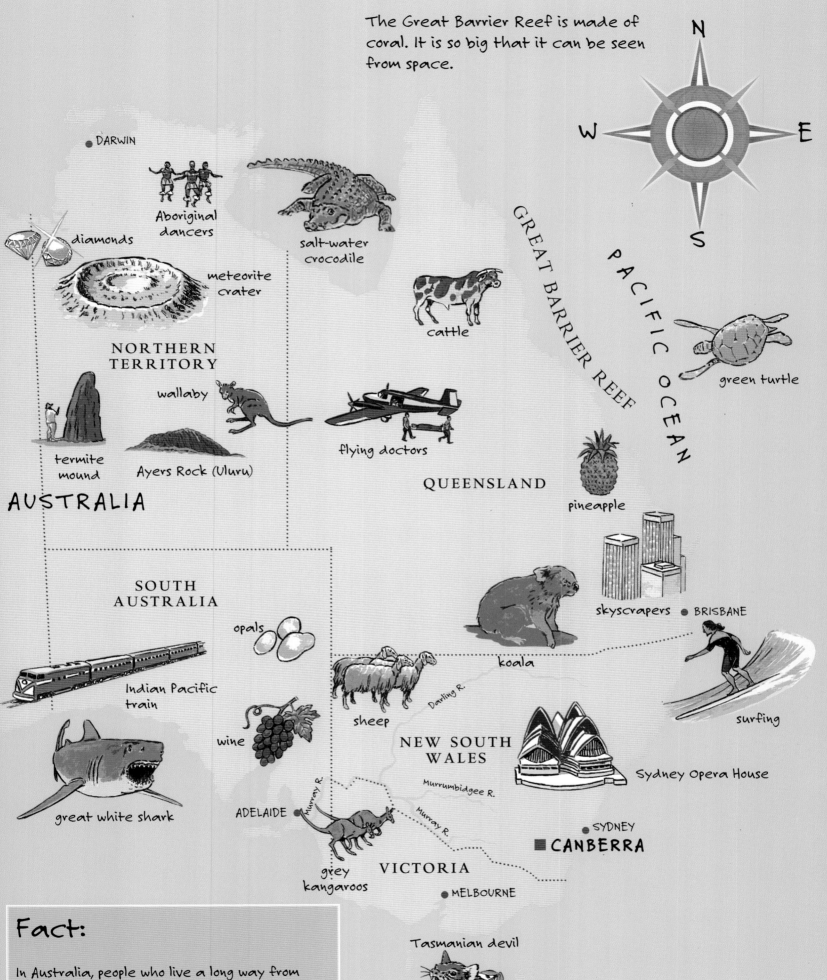

The Great Barrier Reef is made of coral. It is so big that it can be seen from space.

N
W   E
S

DARWIN

diamonds

Aboriginal dancers

salt-water crocodile

meteorite crater

cattle

PACIFIC OCEAN

GREAT BARRIER REEF

green turtle

NORTHERN TERRITORY

wallaby

flying doctors

termite mound

Ayers Rock (Uluru)

QUEENSLAND

pineapple

AUSTRALIA

SOUTH AUSTRALIA

opals

koala

skyscrapers • BRISBANE

Indian Pacific train

great white shark

wine

sheep

Darling R.

surfing

NEW SOUTH WALES

Sydney Opera House

Murrumbidgee R.

Murray R.

ADELAIDE •

Murray R.

• SYDNEY

■ CANBERRA

grey kangaroos

VICTORIA

• MELBOURNE

Fact:

In Australia, people who live a long way from hospitals depend on the Royal Flying Doctor service when they need medical help. The service allows doctors to travel great distances quickly by aeroplane.

Tasmanian devil

TASMANIA
• HOBART

New Zealand

New Zealand is divided into two islands. Most people live on the volcanic North Island. It has large cattle and sheep ranches and exports dairy produce and lamb.

scale

0   50   100   150   200   250 Miles
0   100   200   300   400 Kilometres

kauri tree

kiwi fruit

AUCKLAND

HAMILTON

Maori war dance

oil rig

L. Taupo

NORTH ISLAND

barracuda

Parliament House

WELLINGTON

NEW ZEALAND

N

W   E

S

NEW ZEALAND

TASMAN SEA

SOUTH ISLAND

sheep

Christchurch Cathedral

Rakaia R.

CHRISTCHURCH

sheep

PACIFIC OCEAN

rugby

DUNEDIN

oysters

blue whale

Can you find...

Parliament House?

Christchurch Cathedral?

58

Southwestern Pacific Islands

Thousands of small tropical islands are scattered across the Pacific Ocean east of Australia. Most islanders live in small villages. They fish and grow tropical fruit, including bananas and coconuts.

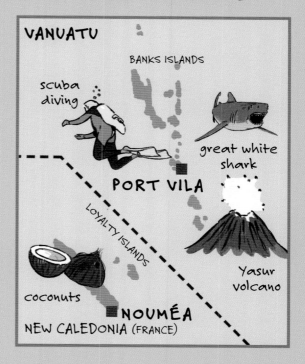

VANUATU

BANKS ISLANDS

scuba diving

great white shark

PORT VILA

LOYALTY ISLANDS

coconuts

Yasur volcano

NOUMÉA

NEW CALEDONIA (FRANCE)

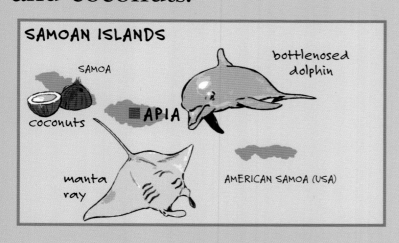

SAMOAN ISLANDS

SAMOA

coconuts

APIA

bottlenosed dolphin

manta ray

AMERICAN SAMOA (USA)

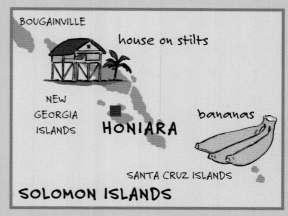

BOUGAINVILLE

house on stilts

NEW GEORGIA ISLANDS

HONIARA

bananas

SANTA CRUZ ISLANDS

SOLOMON ISLANDS

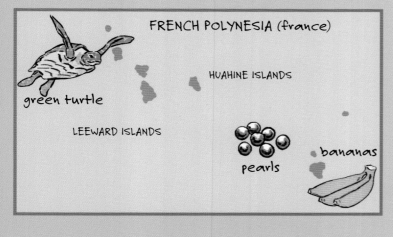

FRENCH POLYNESIA (france)

green turtle

HUAHINE ISLANDS

LEEWARD ISLANDS

pearls

bananas

Fact:

The people of Bougainville in the Solomon Islands have discovered how to use coconut oil as a fuel for cars.

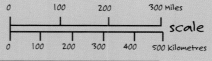

0   100   200   300 Miles

scale

0 100 200 300 400 500 Kilometres

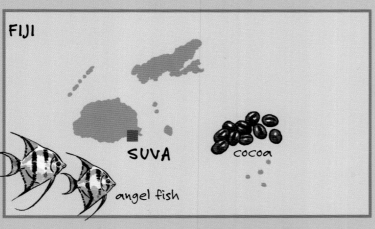

FIJI

SUVA

cocoa

angel fish

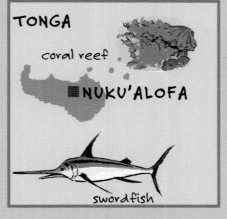

TONGA

coral reef

NUKU'ALOFA

swordfish

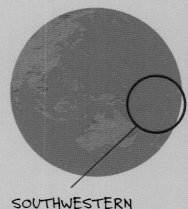

SOUTHWESTERN PACIFIC ISLANDS

The Arctic

The Arctic Ocean is covered in thick ice at the North Pole. The Inuit and Sami are the only people who live in this harsh environment, but many animals and plants survive there.

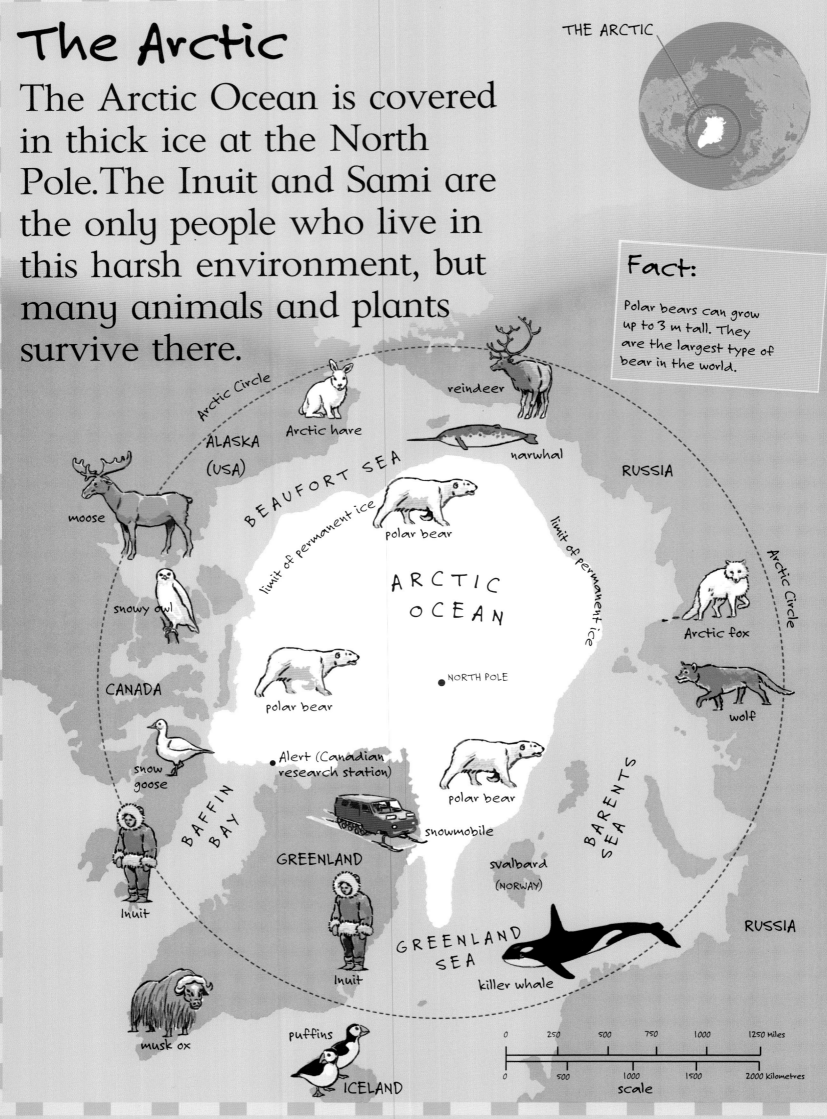

THE ARCTIC

Fact:

Polar bears can grow up to 3 m tall. They are the largest type of bear in the world.

Arctic Circle

Arctic hare

reindeer

ALASKA (USA)

BEAUFORT SEA

narwhal

RUSSIA

moose

limit of permanent ice

polar bear

ARCTIC OCEAN

limit of permanent ice

Arctic Circle

snowy owl

Arctic fox

CANADA

polar bear

NORTH POLE

wolf

snow goose

Alert (Canadian research station)

polar bear

BARENTS SEA

Inuit

BAFFIN BAY

snowmobile

GREENLAND

Svalbard (NORWAY)

RUSSIA

Inuit

GREENLAND SEA

killer whale

musk ox

puffins

ICELAND

| | 0 | 250 | 500 | 750 | 1000 | 1250 Miles |
scale

0   500   1000   1500   2000 Kilometres

The Antarctic

The South Pole in the Antarctic is the coldest place on Earth. No country owns this frozen continent but many have set up scientific research stations there.

0	250	500	750	1000	1250 Miles
0		500	1000	1500	2000 Kilometres

scale

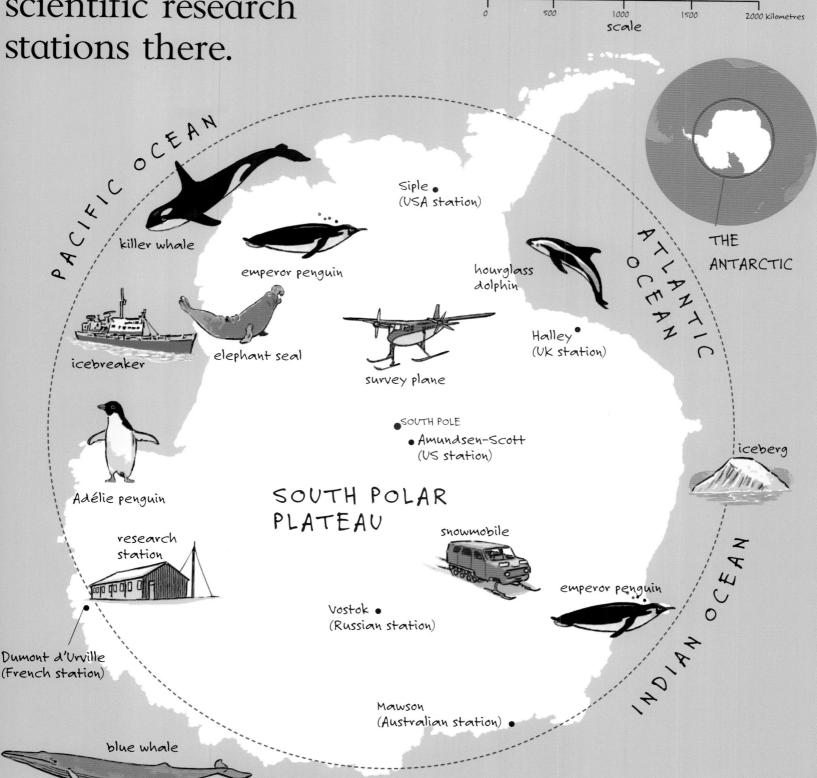

PACIFIC OCEAN

killer whale

emperor penguin

Siple • (USA station)

hourglass dolphin

ATLANTIC OCEAN

THE ANTARCTIC

icebreaker

elephant seal

survey plane

Halley • (UK station)

Adélie penguin

SOUTH POLE • Amundsen-Scott (US station)

iceberg

research station

SOUTH POLAR PLATEAU

snowmobile

emperor penguin

Dumont d'Urville (French station)

Vostok • (Russian station)

INDIAN OCEAN

Mawson (Australian station) •

blue whale

61

Glossary

climate The average weather of a region.

continent One of the large masses of land on the Earth's surface.

desert An area that has very little or no rainfall.

equator The imaginary line around the centre of the Earth. The areas around the equator are the parts of the planet closest to the Sun.

export Something that is sent from one country to be sold in another.

fertile (of soil) Able to grow plenty of crops.

humid Warm and damp.

hurricane A storm with very strong winds.

independence A country ruled by another country gains independence when it begins ruling itself.

latitude Imaginary lines that run horizontally around the Earth.

longitude Imaginary lines that run vertically around the Earth.

magma molten rock beneath the Earth's crust

map projection The process of forming a flat atlas map by 'stretching' a globe.

monsoon A strong South-Asian wind that usually also brings heavy rain.

northern hemisphere The northern half of the Earth above the equator.

peninsula A narrow area of land that sticks out far into the sea.

permanent Likely to last a very long time.

population The people who live in a place or country.

southern hemisphere The southern half of the Earth below the equator.

summit The highest point of a mountain.

tropical Having a very warm and humid climate, as found in the areas around the equator.

volcanic Formed by a volcano.

Index

Editors: Karen Barker Smith
Stephanie Cole

Picture Research: Nicola Roe

Consultant: Penny Clarke

Photographic credits
Digital Stock/Corbis Corporation: 20, 25, 32, 35, 37, 41
John Foxx Images: 29, 31, 43, 45
Pictor International: 10, 17, 26, 51
Salariya Book Company: 15

Published in Great Britain in MMXVI by
Book House, an imprint of
The Salariya Book Company Ltd
25 Marlborough Place, Brighton BN1 1UB
www.salariya.com
www.book-house.co.uk

ISBN: 978-1-910706-11-4

S A L A R I Y A

PAPER FROM
SUSTAINABLE
FORESTS